G000229625

BE̅ ᵢ ᵢ ⌐ ⸝ ᵢ

RUGBY

REFEREEING

Both **Ed Morrison** and **Derek Robinson** grew up in council estates on the edge of Bristol, and each went on to referee many rugby matches. Apart from this, their lives have been totally different. Ed was thrown out of Hartcliffe Comprehensive at the age of sixteen because, although a gifted all-round sportsman, he was learning nothing, while Derek was winning scholar-ships and going on to Cambridge. Ed became an electrician at British Aerospace, while Derek became a novelist. They met at Bristol Rugby Referees' Society, where Derek was revealing a talent for grassroots rugby (the longer the grass, and the deeper the roots, the better) while Ed – despite (he says) a complete lack of ambition – rocketed up the promotion ladder. Within six years he was on the international panel. That was 1989. Since then he has refereed thirty-eight major international matches, including the 1995 Rugby World Cup Final in Johannesburg. Meanwhile, Derek has written a number of books, including *Rugby: A Player's Guide to the Laws*, regularly updated and now in its sixth edition. Derek concedes grudgingly that Ed is the better referee, while Ed is forced to admit that Derek knows a bit about writing.

BETTER
RUGBY
REFEREEING

*Guidance, tips, warnings, insights and
advice on refereeing at every level
of the game*

Ed Morrison and Derek Robinson

WHISTLE BOOKS

*Dedicated to the thousands of referees who give their
services to the game of Rugby Football, for no reason
other than to help thirty players enjoy their
Saturday afternoons*

First published in 1996
by CollinsWillow under the title *Rugby: A Referee's Guide*

This updated edition published in 2007 by
Whistle Books, Bristol, England

**A CIP catalogue record for this book is
available from the British Library**

ISBN 978 0 9555901 0 8

Illustrations by John Gully

Published by Whistle Books, Shapland House, Somerset Street,
Kingsdown, Bristol BS2 8LZ, England

Printed in Great Britain by
Short Run Press Limited, Exeter, Devon

Contents

The Top

Ed Morrison refereed the 1995 Rugby World Cup final between South Africa and New Zealand in Johannesburg. South Africa won 15–12, with a dropped goal in extra time.

Derek: Every referee's dream – and every referee's nightmare – is to be asked to take the Rugby World Cup Final. Along with the greatest honour he can have, comes the risk of cocking-up the biggest game in the world. True?

Ed: True. The appointment was announced to us referees on the Monday before the match, at seven o'clock in the morning. It certainly woke me up very quickly.

Derek: You were surprised?

Ed: Yes. That's not false modesty. There were some very good referees in South Africa for the World Cup, people like Wayne Erickson of Australia and Patrick Robin of France. And take Scotland's Jim Fleming and Ireland's Steven Hilditch and Derek Bevan from Wales – all doing their *third* World Cup. That's huge experience. I knew I was in the running, but . . . I would have been delighted to have been chosen to run the line in the Final, and here they were asking me to take charge of it.

Derek: What happened next?

Ed: Once the initial shock wore off, the next thing that hit me was fear. What if I messed up? What if I made myself look an absolute fool and, worse still, ruined the whole game? In rugby the referee's decision on the field is final; he can't say, 'Hang on, lads, I got that wrong, forget what I said, I've changed my mind.'

Whatever he decides, everyone's stuck with it, so he'd better be right. And he's got a split-second to do it in. So, yes, I felt a bit scared of the prospect.

Derek: How long did that last?

Ed: A few hours. By the Tuesday morning I said to myself: 'Look: this is something that will only happen to you once in your lifetime. Make the most of it.' And I had a positive view, that I was going to enjoy the big day. I stopped worrying. I enjoyed the rest of the week and I certainly enjoyed refereeing the match. Which is how it should be: hard work, but enjoyable.

Derek: But first you had to get through the week. There were a few hundred journalists in Johannesburg . . .

Ed: . . . and they all wanted an interview! The hotel was chock-a-block with people and messages.

Derek: What about television? The Final was carried by 124 countries and some estimates said it was seen by two billion viewers, so I've no doubt a lot of camera crews were trying to get hold of you beforehand.

Ed: Unless you were there, you can't imagine the amount of hype. The pressure was phenomenal, overwhelming. I decided at the start that I wasn't even going to *try* to absorb that pressure. I kept a very low profile all week, so low that I was almost invisible. I spoke to none of the Press. Not one. I gave only one TV interview, and that was pre-arranged with Alistair Hignell for HTV, from Bristol, which is my home town. But that low profile was a wise decision, because everyone and his dog was after me!

Derek: Whatever you do, they'll still write about you. Did you read the papers?

Ed: Some, not all. I know there were very personal attacks on me in the local newspapers, because South Africans kept apologising to me for them. Perhaps it's just as well I didn't see all the papers!

Derek: What were the grounds for these attacks?

Ed: Well, a former player called Uli Schmidt attacked me because

I'd refereed South Africa on four previous occasions, and they'd lost all four games, and I'd sent off a Springbok player, Jamie Small, who was picked for the Final. So Schmidt accused me of being anti-South African. He said I was punishing the country for its apartheid past – all sorts of silly statements that weren't worth responding to. And it all confirmed the wisdom of staying clear of the media.

Derek: What did you do instead?

Ed: I trained hard for three days – an hour and a half session each day. That might not sound much, but it was, for me! Remember the heat and the altitude. Just as well I did train, because of course the game went into extra time. By a stroke of luck, six guys from my club in Bristol, the Quins, were in Johannesburg, and Alan Curtis, a good friend from my playing days, lives there now. So we all met up at his place, socialised quietly, had a look-around, all very relaxed, not too much rugby talk. That helped considerably. Then I heard that the RFU were flying out my wife, Lin, for the Final, which was very pleasing. On the Friday all the referees had an audience with Nelson Mandela – that was a great experience. So the week passed pretty quickly.

Derek: The night before the Final. Sleep well?

Ed: Yes. I had a couple of beers and slept like a log. I never had problems with nerves or lack of sleep or anything. The lovely thing was: all the other referees were very supportive. They seemed almost pleased that I was the lucky one!

THE MATCH

Derek: Now then: the day of the match arrives. Surely you begin to feel the pressure?

Ed: Well . . . yes, but maybe not in the way you mean. There was a problem about Lin's return flight. It had been booked for next day, Sunday, and suddenly the airline cancelled her reservation! Big confusion. I spent all morning on the phone, arguing with officials, and getting angrier and angrier. Eventually it was sorted out. But it certainly took my mind off the match!

Derek: This was at Ellis Park, which is a colossal stadium. Some newcomers find it frightening.

Ed: Luckily I'd already refereed at Ellis Park a few times, so I knew what I was in for. For instance, when I was there before, I gave a try and turned around and saw the massive video screen replaying the try, and immediately I turned away and told myself: *Don't look at it.* Watching that screen might have reduced my concentration on the game. So I was mentally prepared for Ellis Park.

Derek: But were you ready for the intense passion and pressure of that Final?

Ed: I was working flat-out all afternoon, I know that! But I can honestly say I thoroughly enjoyed the match.

Derek: Even that moment when Jonah Lomu got clear of the South African defence and he was certain to score, and you blew for a forward pass that was only inches forward?

Ed: Either a pass is forward or it's not. If I see a forward pass I have no difficulty blowing, no matter who is on the end of it! In 1994, during the Bledisloe Cup in Sydney – a very hard match, very intense – Zinzan Brooke gave Michael Jones what could have been a scoring pass – but I reckoned it was forward and I blew. It's a matter of honesty. Who scores, and who wins, shouldn't come into it. I couldn't enjoy refereeing unless I was absolutely honest about my decisions. Refereeing is all about honesty and enjoyment. If you can't put the first in and get the second out, you shouldn't be doing it.

Scrums

Ed: The scrum is probably the area of the game that makes or breaks a referee.

Derek: Really? More so than, say, the tackle? Or off-side?

Ed: If I feel the scrum is going well, then I feel confident that the game is going well.

Derek: Which is a totally different viewpoint from most spectators, isn't it? They'd probably say the game went well because the ball got thrown about a lot, good tries were scored, not much whistle . . .

Ed: Yes, but none of that will happen if the scrums aren't right to start with. When scrums go wrong, two things happen. First, the ball doesn't get won and so everyone becomes irritated and impatient because no rugby's getting played. And second, the two packs of forwards start getting angry with each other, so that when the ball at last comes out, their anger is carried on to the next phase of play – ruck, or maul, or whatever – and next thing you know, fists are swinging, all because of the scrum. So it's essential that the referee gets the scrum working properly from the very start.

Derek: How do you set about it? What's your formula?

Ed: I work hard on the first scrums to make sure they stick to the sequence of engagement: the way the two front rows come together. Before the match, when I'm in the dressing rooms to check the studs, I call the entire front rows together and the front-row replacements and I spell out how I'm going to manage the scrums. I say: 'I will give you a mark with my foot. Don't shove beyond the mark before the ball's put in, or you're liable to be penalised.' Then I move on to the engagement.

Derek: Used to be a three-stage process. Now it's four-stage.

Ed: And every referee, at every level, *must* follow it. No variations.

Derek: Crouch–Touch–Pause–Engage. What does each stage mean?

Ed: 'Crouch' means both front rows have horizontal backs, they're at the same level and looking at each other. 'Touch' means each prop briefly touches his opposing prop's shoulder. This establishes the correct distance between front rows. Too far apart, there's a risk of injury when they hit. 'Pause' gives the referee a chance to make a final check – everyone bound, everything square and tight and tidy. Then 'Engage' is permission – not a command – to the front rows to come together. That's the sequence. Done properly, it means far fewer scrum collapses.

Derek: What if a team engages too soon?

Ed: You blow up immediately. They're trying to anticipate your 'Engage', to get an advantage with an early shove. That's a Free Kick offence. I'm constantly telling referees of the Fear Factor, meaning if they don't manage the scrum engagement properly they should be afraid, be very afraid, because they're in big trouble! I referee the first few scrums quite hard. Certainly at the senior level they're very confrontational. Those guys have got steam coming out of their ears. It's their chance to test their strength.

Derek: At a big game, if there's an early punch-up . . .

Ed: . . . it's usually at the first one or two scrums. That's when the referee must work hard on *managing the engagement* of the scrum. If he lets them engage in their own sweet way, *they* are managing *him*. He's lost control. And once you lose control, it's ten times harder to get it back.

ENGAGEMENT OF SCRUM

Derek: Okay. It's the first scrum, the forwards are assembling. What d'you want from them?

Ed: I want everyone legally bound, to start with. Especially I want the props tightly bound on their hooker and the hooker getting a good grip on his props. If he can't reach their armpits, I want to see him get two good fistfuls of jersey. As the scrum forms up, I'll say: 'Two units.' Meaning, nothing happens until the second row has added itself. Then the back row binds on. I make sure all eight are properly bound. I want the two halves of the scrum facing each other squarely – not angled across the pitch. All these things go toward building a strong scrum.

Derek: Essential, with up to half a ton of beef making contact.

Ed: At senior level, I like the front rows to hit hard, because when they hit hard, the engagement is *tight*. You can only do this with technically sound players. Sometimes you hear the crowd go: 'Ohhhh . . .' when the scrum goes THUD! But there's nothing wrong with it. They all know where they're going, they hit, their shoulders take the pressure and the scrum's *locked tight*. What I don't like is when they just flop in. It makes the scrum very loose. Some props prefer that. Jeff Probyn, the great England prop, did. He told me he didn't like the scrum to engage with a bang. He wanted the freedom to burrow, and to work on his opposite number. He didn't want the hard impact, bang! I do. In my opinion it makes the scrum a lot more stable.

Derek: Okay. Now, down in the grassroots where I referee, I won't let the front rows engage until the scrum-half's alongside me and ready to put the ball in.

Ed: Right. We must control the scrum, and that includes the scrum-half.

Derek: And as soon as they engage, I make him get on with it.

Ed: Right again.

Derek: And the scrum doesn't collapse.

Ed: I remember Clive Norling saying to me: 'One reason the lawmakers keep tinkering with the laws on the scrum is because it's refereed poorly.' That's a relevant and fair criticism. If we do it right – if we keep them apart until the scrum-half's ready, then they engage hard and tight, then the ball's in reasonably quickly – we'll have fewer collapsed scrums.

Derek: Yet you still see, even in internationals, the referee let the scrum engage while the scrum-half's off searching for the ball.

Ed: That referee's in trouble. We must never forget the scrum law just to satisfy a player. Mike Fry, the Bristol prop, disliked waiting so much that he used to say: 'Just let us get in.' I told him to stay where he was. He wanted to make his opposition as uncomfortable as possible before the put-in.

Derek: Of course, after they engage, that can be done quite legally, can't it? You see games in which one front row is put under heavy pressure.

Ed: It's a private game up there. Provided the scrummaging remains safe, I wouldn't interfere, because it's an integral part of the game. The only time I get worried about front rows is when one is so much stronger than the other that it's not really a contest any more. Then I might ask players to back off a little.

Derek: Even at senior level?

Ed: Yes. I remember when Bath were playing Toulouse. 'Cooch' (Gareth Chilcott) was at tight-head, and he had the French loose-head in such trouble, he didn't know what day it was. I could see the front rows were becoming very messy, so at every scrum I was saying, 'Back off, Cooch, back off.' Which he did: just eased the pressure on this poor guy a bit. Then Bath had a scrum very near the Toulouse goal line. Before I could speak, Cooch said: 'Don't you ask me to back off now.'

Derek: So you've got to pick your spot.

Ed: Right. If the players have confidence in you, you can ask them to back off a little in midfield. Near the goal line it's different. I know front rows work tirelessly, but they really put in the maximum effort when they're five or ten metres from the goal line. The first couple of scrums in a match may be full of confrontation, but if the referee can manage them successfully, he's won the players' confidence and the front rows usually settle down to a degree of compromise.

Derek: What if the very first scrum is such a battlefield that you've got to lecture them?

Ed: I never give a lecture at the first scrum. I've done my lecturing in the dressing room. If there's a problem, the most I'll say is: 'Look, guys, you're all experienced players. You don't need lectures from me. But either you play the game or we're all going to have problems.'

Derek: That's probably as much information as they're capable of absorbing.

Ed: Exactly. They're all pumped-up, ready for battle, the last thing they want to hear is this prat of a referee giving them a lecture on how to play the front row. So don't do it! They're not listening! There's absolutely no point in talking to anybody who's not listening. One of the things that new referees have to learn is this: if you're going to do anything about penalising scrums, do it early, because if players aren't listening, maybe they'll understand a penalty. I see lots of referees, often at the very first scrum, standing *between* the front rows, holding them apart, which is the most dangerous place for the referee to be.

Derek: He's the nut in the nutcrackers.

Ed: Yes. He's giving this wonderful lecture on front-row play and nobody's listening. They just want to get in! It's suicidal. What's more, front-row players don't like to be touched, by the referee or the opposition. It's one of those macho things.

Derek: I used to be a prop. We're very sensitive people.

Ed: I've noticed. I *never* touch the front rows.

Derek: At junior level, sometimes their self-control fails. They engage too soon.

Ed: At senior level, too. If a team goes in too early, I penalise. And if they *don't* go in, I penalise.

Derek: What for?

Ed: Engaging too early is delaying the scrum. Free Kick offence.

Ed: Here's a nut in a nutcracker. The referee should never stand between the front rows. He should never lay hands on them. He should never deliver long lectures, especially at the first scrums. These front rows are getting impatient. Any moment now, this referee will get squashed.

Derek: That's interesting. Presumably it's the other team's put-in?

Ed: Yes. New Zealand do it very well. It's not necessarily the whole front row who don't go in.

Derek: So if they engage, but the hooker's head is still in the air . . .

Ed: They're playing for time. They want to frustrate the opposition slightly. Suppose you've got a situation where, out of six guys, five go in and one doesn't – penalise him.

Derek: No excuse for it?

Ed: Certainly not at senior level. When they engage, it's usually the tight-head who leads. Sometimes the hooker. He'll say: 'Hit!' And the others all go in on his lead. If a player doesn't, it's probably deliberate. And if it happens early in the game and you penalise that guy, he gets the message very quickly. They might think: *I don't like this referee – but he's on top of the game.*

Derek: In the 1996 Bledisloe Cup game at Wellington, you penalised Australia for not engaging at the very first scrum.

**MIDDLE
LINE**

Ed: This shows how the props should bind on their opponents – high on the shoulder, not on the upper arms. When a prop binds legally, he can't pull his opponent down with the outside arm. The loose-head prop's left arm must be inside the tight-head's right arm. Referees should visualise this: straight backs and proper binding.

Ed: Yes, straight from the kick-off. New Zealand ran the ball and scored a try virtually in the first minute of the match.

Derek: The weather was foul, wasn't it? But the rugby was brilliant. Good scrummaging must have helped.

Ed: It's all a matter of *managing* the engagement of the scrum correctly and well. You're in control. What's really frustrating is when you've done all that but the scrum-half waits and waits and waits for the tap.

Derek: The tap being the hooker's signal?

Ed: To put the ball in. Maybe he's uncomfortable, the opposition's got him under a bit of pressure, so he waits. You've got to penalise that delay, too. Interestingly, it hardly ever happens in France. The French do the quick feed very well. They might chuck it in the second row as the scrum engages, but they get it in!

Derek: We've been talking about senior rugby. What about junior games? If you were refereeing a school match, would you be as strict on this business of delay?

Ed: When a front-row player fails to engage, maybe it's from lack of skill – or maybe he's trying to waste time or spoil the opposition's shove. I might give him one chance – but next time, I'd penalise.

Ed: At schoolboy level I would manage the scrums even more firmly, because they haven't got the same strength in the upper body and neck as the older guys, or the same technical skill, so the risk of injury is greater and it's even more important that the scrums are managed well. If the hooker's head stays up, I might say: 'You've got one chance – and you've just had your chance. If you don't engage when everyone else does, I'm going to penalise you.' Another thing I want is for the front rows to engage with their heads braced and looking up, not dipped and looking down.

Sometimes you get a team that's weak in the front rows, maybe the impact frightens them slightly, they dip their heads, their backs aren't straight.

Derek: That's a big problem in women's rugby. Not enough upper-body strength.

Ed: At international level they've improved a lot. I tell players, 'It's in your interests and your safety to look up when you engage.' If I saw the hooker's head bent and looking at the ground, I might break up the scrum or else I'd certainly tell him before the next scrum, 'If you don't engage looking up again, we're going to have a problem.'

Derek: Okay. They engage, the ball's put in. What are your priorities now?

Ed: I want a fair contest for the ball, and then fair use of possession once the ball's been won. In fact that's what I want in *every* area of the game.

Derek: But maybe the scrum's more important. It's the *only* area where a team can be reasonably sure of winning the ball on their put-in.

Ed: Unless they're very technically inferior, they should win it every time. At international level, a strike against the head normally means the ball's been accidentally kicked through – although the hooker obviously takes the credit! But at every level, all sorts of things *can* go wrong. Primarily, I want the scrum to *stay* a scrum – not to collapse or disintegrate before the team that's won the ball has done what it wants with it. So I'm looking out for props who try to drag the opposition down, and I'm looking to see that nobody breaks his binding before the scrum ends, and about twenty other things.

Derek: Such as what?

Ed: For instance, in a good scrum the shove by both teams is forward. The player's backs are parallel. They're all tightly bound. If a tight-head prop's body starts to angle – so the hips move outwards – then his head may be going *inward* and boring into the opposing hooker's head. Very painful. Look at the prop's left arm. As he angles out, he probably slips his binding on his hooker. Boring like this also lets him put a terrific strain on the opposing loose-head's right shoulder. It might even split the front row wide open. Next thing you know, fists are flying. If the hooker slips his binding, it's often because he's in trouble and he's trying to reach farther and faster when he strikes. Or it may be that the opposing front row are so low, the hooker can't

Ed: One reason for scrum collapses is boring by the tight-head prop – usually on the referee's blind side. Tell-tale signs are: the tight-head prop's hips swing out, allowing his head to angle in and bore on the opposing hooker. The prop's binding slips. Boring can split a scrum apart and make it collapse.

see the put-in, in which case you need to get them higher – penalising the hooker won't solve the problem. You need to check the tunnel. Sometimes the defending tight-head will have his head down where it blocks the hooker's view.

Derek: I remember taking a game where the tight-head's hair was so long that it almost reached the ground. Fashions have changed since then, thank God.

Ed: You've got to be alert to everything. After a successful strike, the other hooker may attempt a kamikaze swing with one leg, or even both legs, which is highly dangerous. His foot gets trapped and he's helpless. Anything's possible. I learnt one lesson the difficult way. I won't say which international side it was, but they used to deliberately take down the scrum on the opposition's put-in. Collapsed it on the blind side. They enticed the referee – me – around to that side, where I couldn't see the put-in, at least not very well. Then, as the scrum-half went to put the ball in, the defending scrum-half knocked the ball out of his hands and into *his* side of the scrum.

Derek: Unbelievable.

Ed: *The splitting scrum is a recent phenomenon, but we're seeing it happen more and more. This illustration is typical. Blacks win the heel and shove the White scrum back. To stop this, the White front row unbinds and stands up. Pressure is still on from the Black scrum, so its front row slides across the White front row, and the scrum splits in half. This means it's no longer a scrum – but unless the referee blows up at once, the Black pack is quite likely to rumble on and take the ball upfield.*

Ed: And that was a coached, planned move by one of the most senior rugby nations in the world. It taught me a lesson. Sometimes you *need* to visit the other side of the scrum, just to introduce yourself to the other props and ask them if they're enjoying their afternoon; but now I always use my touch judges if I can, to watch the feed. Because I always remember being conned *once.*

Derek: I suppose that must be a good example of what you mean by 'fair contest for the ball'. What about fair use of possession?

Ed: Collapsing used to be the big worry. It wasted possession because the referee had to blow up. Now they're standing up much more often – and stopping the opposition's drive. In law, a scrum that stands up is classified as a collapse.

Derek: This is the front row you're talking about.

Ed: Yes. The ball's been heeled and held, that team gets a shove on, and suddenly the opposing front row stands up. They're no longer bound to the other team. The laws say that unless the two front rows are bound, it's not a scrum and the referee must blow up and re-set the scrum. The result is, the team that had a drive on loses that advantage. I'm not happy about this.

Derek: Why did the front row do it? Did they deliberately stand, or were they popped up by their opponents?

Ed: That's for the referee to decide. Sometimes, of course, it happens accidentally. But front rows are getting quite good at it, especially in New Zealand. If, as a referee, you read the situation and decide a player is simply standing up to abort the drive, you've got to do something about it. If you decide his opponents deliberately 'popped' him up, that's dangerous play, of course. It's all part of the difficult decisions a referee has to make.

Derek: People say the line-out is a jungle, but the front row is a minefield.

Ed: It can be. You do get the odd game when – for whatever reason, maybe an old feud, or something that happened last year, because props never forget, you see, they've got fantastic memories – the red mist comes down in front of their eyes, they won't listen, and you've got a problem. But front rows aren't stupid. Usually they can create a sort of peaceful co-existence. Provided there's not too much friction, I'm a great believer in not getting too involved. Scrummaging is a specialist affair, and if they can enjoy a good contest without affecting everybody else, I'm happy to let them get on with it. I certainly don't go looking for trouble.

Derek: The key words there are 'without affecting everybody else'. What did you have in mind?

Ed: Leaving aside things like collapsing and standing, which are obviously bad news for everyone, I go back to the question of ensuring good use of possession. The law says that each team must have all eight players in a scrum, and all eight must be bound to it at all times. That includes the back row: both flankers and the No. 8. And because none of the opposition's players can break their binding until the ball is out of the scrum, the team that's won possession should be guaranteed a certain space and time to use the ball in, without being hassled.

Derek: Except by the opposing scrum-half.

Ed: Exactly. So I want to see flankers properly bound, not just holding on with two fingers, because that means they're creeping forward, trying to close down the other team's space when the ball comes out. For the same reason I don't want the props or the locks to break *their* binding while the ball's in the scrum. If the prop disengages from his opposite number, it makes the scrum such an untidy mess. We've got to keep that area of the game clean – above all for safety reasons. Either I penalise it immediately or – if an advantage is gained by the opponents – at the next opportunity, I say to the prop: 'Don't break your binding until the scrum's over.' I've warned the locks, too.

Derek: You're talking about the team *not* in possession?

Ed: Yes. What we're seeing more and more of is a team losing the strike, getting shunted back until its front row breaks its binding and slides away, disengages altogether.

Derek: Is that legal?

Ed: Each team must have eight players in the scrum, and that means bound onto it with the full arm. Flankers, of course, are often tempted to slip their binding in order to gain a yard or two – especially when they're on the referee's blind side.

Ed: It can't be. What happens, it's normally a channelled ball back to the No. 8. They crab the scrum sideways, and when the opposition front row break their bindings, the half of the scrum in possession just walks away with the ball at the No. 8's feet. I'd blow up immediately.

Derek: Well, let's define the offence.

Ed: You can penalise one team for breaking their binding. If you don't think they did it deliberately, then all those opponents walking away are in front of the ball and, at the very least, offside, if not obstructing their opponents.

Derek: What would you do?

Ed: I'd blow up as soon as a team broke their binding. What I *wouldn't* do is let them walk away for twenty metres, and *then* blow up. The crowd would ask what the hell was going on – and quite right, too!

Derek: This walking-away stunt brings back memories. There was a time, long ago, when wheeling the scrum was a respectable tactic. The scrum got wheeled one way and the second row broke free with the ball at their feet. Scotland were brilliant at it. Of course, in those days a scrum need have only three from each team in it.

Ed: Whereas now it's eight. It's a funny thing, wheeling. I think it's the next thing the lawmakers will change.

Derek: It's not illegal. Except at Under-19 level.

Ed: It's not illegal, and the controlled wheel is a good attacking ploy. It takes the ball away from the opposing scrum-half, and it can also swing the back row around so that they're closer to the goal line. What's changed everything in recent years is the turnover. Wheel 90 degrees and win possession. Or, if a team wheels less than 90, disrupt their opponents' possession. The one man who can frustrate an attempted wheel is the tight-head prop. He must be strong and competent. Good tight-heads are a very rare breed indeed. Top coaches tell me that a good tight-head should be the highest-paid player!

Derek: So what is he up against? What's the secret of the wheel?

Ed: Let's look at three basic actions. Obviously the defending team – not in possession of the ball – is trying to wheel, because they want the turnover. And ideally they want to wheel the scrum clockwise.

Derek: Turning it anti-clockwise would just give the opposing scrum-half extra protection from his back row?

Ed: Sure. So, first of all, the defending forwards concentrate all their attention on the far side of the front row, against their opponents' tight-head. They pack maximum power against him. If they can shove him backwards, they're in business. So that's when a good tight-head is invaluable. Secondly, their back row swings to the left, to increase the wheel. I've seen back-row players cross their feet as the scrum rotates! Like a chorus line. And thirdly, the defending tight-head pulls with his outside arm and tries to step back. If he's successful, the attacking loose-head goes forward while the attacking tight-head is going back, and Bingo! The wheel picks up speed. Now it's hard to stop.

Derek: But not entirely legal, surely.

Ed: That third move – a prop pulling his opponent – is totally illegal. So the key for the referee is deciding: is the wheel done legally or illegally? Which is not to say that every legal wheel is safe. If a scrum suddenly spins, the whip effect on a player's neck can be bad news.

Derek: You're not a great fan of wheeling, are you?

Ed: I'd like the scrum to get back to its first principle, which is that you shove me and I'll shove you. I like the Definition in the scrum law: 'The purpose of the scrum is to restart play quickly, safely and fairly . . .' Wheeling isn't restarting play, it's stopping play, and I don't like the idea of rewarding a team for stopping play.

Derek: And maybe killing time.

Ed: Possibly. A team leading by only a couple of points. Dying minutes.

Derek: If I were to guess what's on the IRB's mind, I'd say it's ways to eliminate time-wasting. Rugby players have shown an amazing ability to cock-up the scrum. Back in the 1930s they invented 'run-around', which was a running battle to get the loose-head advantage. If your opponents had it, your prop on the far side broke free, ran around, bound on and became the *new* loose-head – until an opponent ran around and stole it back, and so on. Scrums crabbed halfway across the field. Colossal time-wasting.

Ed: Referees need to be alert to players' intent. We've got to make the scrum work. It's one reason we get people of all shapes and sizes in rugby. There's talk of de-powering the scrum, taking the contest out of it, and I think that would be disastrous.

WHEN IS THE SCRUM OVER?

Derek: Okay. Now, I've saved the worst bit for last. When is the ball out of the scrum?

Ed: It's out when the referee decides it's out.

Derek: True. But – unless you're going to announce when it's out, that's not much help to the opposing scrum-half, is it? The ball may look well and truly out to him but if you disagree, he's given away a penalty. And the Lawbook isn't much help. It rabbits on at great length about putting the ball *in*, but as for how and when it's *out* – that's something we're all assumed to know by instinct.

Ed: It's an area that new referees often have a lot of trouble with.

Derek: Well, let's try to define the problem. Ken Rowlands – who's a former international referee – was asked the question, and he said, 'The ball's out when a bird can shit on it.' Do you agree?

Ed: Yes and no.

Derek: You mean it depends on the size of the bird?

Ed: No, it's a bit more complicated than that. Let's begin by looking at the various channels. Where can the ball legally come out? If it pops out between a prop's feet, or between a prop and the flanker binding on him, there's usually no question – it's obviously out, and anybody can have it. Usually, of course, it's heeled through the back row.

Derek: So now we're looking at these three guys' legs. Suppose the ball gets heeled out *between* the legs of a flanker?

Ed: Once it's clear of his feet, it's out. The scrum's over. Anyone can play it. The same with the No. 8: once it's behind his feet, it's out. And of course if the No. 8 unbinds with the ball at his feet, the scrum's over.

Ed: The scrum ends when the ball is out – but when is that? I draw an imaginary line that links the feet of the back row. As long as the ball is inside this 'webbed' area, I reckon the scrum-half of that team can have it but the opposing scrum-half can't. As soon as the scrum-half handles the ball, he's fair game – now the scrum has ended and anyone can tackle him.

Derek: We need to be absolutely clear about this, because the law says that a player must not handle the ball in the scrum. And that includes the scrum-half.

Ed: Correct.

Derek: If the No. 8 is still bound-on, with the ball in front of his feet, and the scrum-half picks it out, I always penalise. I say the ball must come back to him – he can't go in for it.

Ed: I agree. If we don't draw a clear line, we're going to have the scrum-half reaching into the second row for the ball. That's not what the scrum's about.

Derek: Right. Now we get down to routine possession. Nine times out of ten, the ball comes out through the gap between a flanker and the No. 8. That's quite a big gap.

Ed: Oh, yes. It could easily be a yard wide.

Derek: Using Ken Rowlands' test, big enough for a buzzard to hit from a hundred feet.

Ed: Yes.

Derek: So, once the ball's been heeled into that gap, it's out of the scrum. I mean, you wouldn't penalise the team's scrum-half for picking it up?

Ed: No, certainly not.

Derek: Suppose the opposing scrum-half grabbed it?

Ed: I'd penalise him.

Derek: You and ten thousand other referees. Yet the laws specifically say that any player who is onside can pick up the ball. And this player is clearly onside. He can't be offside because there's no scrum offside line. How do we know that? Because you've already said the referee wouldn't penalise the other scrum-half for handling the ball, so that means it must be out of the scrum, which means the scrum is over. No scrum, no scrum offside. Yet the player's penalised. Does any of this make sense?

Ed: Yes and no.

Derek: Because it sounds to me like a severe case of double standards.

Ed: That depends on how you look at the situation. I think it's a matter of using a degree of commonsense to solve a problem. This team has won possession. The question is, how to let them *use* that possession and get the ball into play as tidily as possible.

Derek: I see. Well, if that's the question, it seems to me that the answer is to give special privileges to one scrum-half.

Ed: It starts with the scrum offside law. The scrum-half of the team that's won the ball can put one foot in front of it and be onside. His opposite number can't, so his freedom's restricted. And if you mentally draw a line through a back row's feet, when the ball's in front of it the first scrum-half can take it but his opponent can't.

Derek: So referees have created a sort of Exclusion Zone?

Ed: Yes, if you like.

Derek: Let's not tap-dance around the conclusion, because it's pretty obvious, isn't it? We're favouring one scrum-half against the other. We're saying to one guy, the ball's out and you can handle it, at the same time that we tell the other guy, sorry, it's *not* out and if you touch it we'll penalise you.

Ed: There's no doubt that the offside law allows one team a very considerable advantage. It's another of those practicalities which can't be justified by the Lawbook, but it's been considered essential in order to get the ball away quickly and cleanly from the base of the scrum.

Derek: The essence of the situation is that one player is getting preferential treatment, at the expense of the other player.

Ed: Yes. In order to create a tidy package and move the ball. It's commonsense refereeing.

Derek: That's fine. Just as long as we all know what's going on.

Ed: I think both scrum-halves usually understand what's happening. At senior level there's no problem. At junior level the referee might need to communicate, to stop the opposing scrum-half giving away needless penalties. In my experience when a problem arises in this area of the game it's usually because the opposing scrum-half has got himself into that sort of no-man's-land between the left-hand flanker and the No. 8. I dread that. To be honest, I wish the back row would simply move the ball over to the right.

Derek: If they work the ball into the channel between the No. 8 and the right-hand flanker, their scrum-half is fireproof, isn't he?

Ed: It's the safest channel. The opposing scrum-half can't get past the No. 8 without going offside.

Derek: In fact, if the left-hand flanker's got long legs, it's often quite difficult for the opposing scrum-half to get past *his* feet and stay onside.

Ed: Yes – especially when that flanker packs close to the scrum. When he packs at a wide angle, he creates a very large space between himself and his No. 8. I don't think he can claim all that room to hide the ball in. And if the opposing scrum-half can get himself into that angle, he can make a great nuisance of himself, quite legally.

Scrum Collapse

Derek: Two things about collapsed scrums. Firstly, the game's better than it was ten or fifteen years ago, when collapsing was a plague. Secondly, it's still an eyesore and a reason to worry.

Ed: What concerns me is that a couple of times a season every referee gets a game where the front rows decide to have their little private battle and make it a nightmare for everyone involved. No matter what the referee does – you can blow a penalty every scrum – the red mist comes down and they won't listen. It happens at every level.

Derek: England versus Western Samoa in 1995? Eighty minutes of collapsing scrums.

Ed: Not a great advertisement for rugby. Obviously it's up to the referee to do all he can to correct it – but the players have got a big responsibility too. Open rugby means entertaining rugby. If players at the top level expect to be paid, they can't go on sabotaging the scrum.

Derek: It's boring.

Ed: People won't pay to see it. And what worries me is if players don't make a success of the scrum, then the lawmakers might de-power it, turn it into something like a Rugby League scrum, which is no scrum at all. We don't want that. The scrum's an integral part of rugby. It can be marvellous. I'll never forget Ireland against France in the 1995 World Cup. Ireland were beaten, they knew they weren't going to win. In the last 20 minutes, France really put the pressure on. They had three or four scrums on the Irish line, French put-in. I thought: pushover try, for sure. But Garry Halpin, the tight-head prop, and the whole Irish front row just *dug in*. I could *hear* them, groaning and grunting, they were *not* going to be driven back. And they weren't! They didn't collapse. They dug in. Afterwards I said to their coach, Gerry Murphy, 'What a brilliant piece of scrummaging! You've lost the game, you're tired, you're playing in 80 degrees of heat, you're a long way from home – and yet you've still got the balls to *hang in*. That was tremendous, a little piece of poetry.' It's something we don't want to lose. But if the players keep messing it up, we might.

Derek: So what's going on? Which players are causing the trouble? And how?

Ed: We've got to distinguish between senior and junior rugby. At the top level the players are good at knowing the collapse is coming, being ready, and going down on their knees so that nobody gets hurt. They have strength and technique and experience. Junior players often lack all three. If a youngster playing in the front row doesn't know *how* to fall, he hits the ground with the top of his head, he's all doubled-up and the shove is still on from his second row, and *that's* when he might get hurt. Most neck injuries from collapsed scrums involve young lads. That's why referees must blow up the instant the front rows go down. But if the referee manages the scrum properly – tight binding, heads up, shoulders up, backs arched, quick put-in – the scrum should *never* go down, even on a wet day, unless one front row is far stronger and their opponents just fall apart under the pressure. That's when you've got a big problem.

Derek: You can't penalise players for being strong. Or weak.

Ed: Certainly not. But you can talk to players, ask them to back off. Scrum on the halfway line: you might say, 'Don't put so much effort in, back off slightly' Some of the guys look at you as if to say, 'You must be joking.' And if it's a loose-head winning his first international cap, he wants to impress, he's *never* going to back off. But predominantly the guys will be helpful – provided they've got confidence in you. When a side is so *dominant* that it becomes embarrassing, nobody really enjoys that. Talk to the players, and if they won't co-operate, talk to the captains. Shift some of the burden onto *them*, see if they can come up with an answer. If Plan A doesn't work, look for Plan B. Find a solution. But do something, or the problem will just get worse and worse.

Derek: Suppose it's a junior game, Under-19 for instance, and suppose nothing you do makes any difference. You've penalised them, you've talked to the front rows, you've involved the captains – and *still* the scrums collapse. You're well into the second half of the match. And you're getting worried.

Ed: So you should be! At this rate, somebody could get hurt.

Derek: But short of abandoning the match, what more can you do?

Ed: Tell the captains you consider it dangerous to continue with the status quo and you're introducing uncontested scrums.

Derek: You might have to explain what status quo means.

Ed: But the truth is, you should never allow yourself to get into this situation. The match is well into its second half, isn't it? So the problem should have been sorted out long ago. The best way to solve a really bad problem is to tackle it before it reaches that stage! Don't let it become really bad. Work harder, sooner. It pays off later.

Derek: Suppose the scrums only *start* collapsing in the second half?

Ed: Then you've got to find out why. This is an Under-19 match, so it could be sheer fatigue.

Derek: Maybe one of the props has hurt his shoulder.

Ed: Well then, talk to the captain. Try and get him replaced. If there's nobody available who's fit to play in the front row, you've got to go to uncontested scrums. They might not like it, but that's not your fault. It's up to the teams to field players suitably trained and competent to scrimmage. If they don't, they can't have scrums. Obvious.

Derek: Agreed. Now, at senior level, why do scrums collapse? Assuming they engage with a bang and they're all locked in tight?

Ed: Not every scrum collapse is dangerous – but this one is. An experienced front row will go down on its knees. Here, the Black front row has fallen head-first. The pressure from the Black second row is still on. There is serious risk of injury to the back, shoulders, neck or head. What caused the collapse? Almost certainly wrong body-positions or slack binding, made worse, perhaps, by fatigue, wet conditions – or foul play.

Ed: I'm convinced that sometimes they don't know themselves who's collapsing it. And remember: not every collapsed scrum is deliberately collapsed. Sometimes it just happens. A player might even say, 'Sorry, ref – I slipped,' and it's the truth. So the referee shouldn't go looking to penalise every collapse. But there are giveaway signs to look for. Front rows like to get *under* the opposition. If they dip too low, bang goes their straight shove. As soon as the power comes on, down they go. If they slip their bindings, the front row loses its nice tight solidity, down they go. If a prop tries to bore, his body-angle's all wrong, he makes the scrum so uncomfortable that it can't stay up. The best advice for a new referee is to have played in the front row. Then he'll know! If you never played in the scrum, talk to some forwards, listen to what they say. It pays to have some understanding of what makes these guys tick, their psychology. When I was young and I played in the scrum, the older guys told me, 'If things get uncomfortable, go down and start again.' Because a front row hates to be driven back five yards and *then* have to collapse. It hurts their feelings! They'd sooner drop it at the start – and of course you've got to penalise that.

Derek: If you can spot it.

Ed: Exactly. And I often say to the front rows: 'Don't try to con a conner.' They'll con you if they can. Let's face it, scrums are a very easy area for somebody to try and con three points out of you, especially within kicking range of goal. I've had games where I've made it clear I knew what was going on.

Derek: Really? At what level?

Ed: Usually senior level. Obviously, I wouldn't leave it at that. I'd get them back up and say: 'Look – *you're* looking for a penalty, *you're* looking for a penalty, and neither of you are having one.' And I'd try to get some sense into them. What often happens is we get referees who penalise when they are not sure. I've often been criticised, people have said, 'You didn't penalise the front row.' And I say, 'No, I couldn't see who was collapsing. To me, they were each as guilty as the other. It was a personal duel.' Other referees might say: 'Right: I'll penalise *you* this time and penalise *you* next time.' But that's not solving the problem.

Derek: And it might decide the result of the match.

Ed: If there's a goal-kicker like Ronan O'Gara on the park, it might well do. Giving penalties when you don't *know* – to me, that's basically cheating. I'm a great advocate of *never* penalising unless I'm *convinced* I know who's responsible. I say: Let's *manage* the scrum. If you consistently penalise a team from the first to the eightieth minute, you've not solved the problem.

Derek: One cause of collapsing is obvious. We can all see it on television: the props try to drag each other down. The tension in their arms is obvious. Mind you, they're invariably on the blind side.

Ed: True.

Derek: And the referee goes to the blind side and they stop doing it. He goes away and they start again.

Ed: Very often what I'll do is break up the scrum and say to the props on the far side: 'I've just instructed the touch judge to flag the next man who pulls down, or bores in, or whatever.' You've got to pick your moment to do this. Do it when you're five

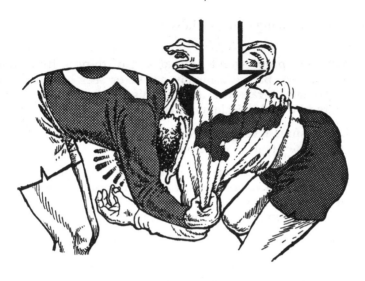

Ed: If a prop can pull down his opponent, he can disrupt the opposition's shove and maybe force them to collapse. Here, the Black tight-head prop has grabbed his opponent's sleeve and dragged his arm down so far that his upper body is twisted and he can no longer bind with either arm. This spells trouble – either collapse or possibly retaliation.

metres from touch, so that the touch judge can hear you, and so can everybody else.

Derek: And you find that works.

Ed: Sometimes. The point is, it's another way to *manage* the scrum. Your touch judge can be very helpful. The most callous thing I've seen in front-row play in recent years was when a flanker grabbed the opposing prop's leg. That's a cautioning offence, if not a sending-off. Imagine the strength of those guys, the power they're generating – if someone takes your leg away just as the weight comes on, you're in serious trouble.

Derek: That was in a top game?

Ed: An international, the Bledisloe Cup. It was flagged by the touch judge, I cautioned the New Zealand flanker straight away. Sean Fitzpatrick, his captain, had no gripe at me – he said he wouldn't like it done to him!

Derek: It's amazing, isn't it, how many ways the players can think of to cock up a good game?

Ed: Normally props won't do that sort of thing – they won't stoop that low. But occasionally a flanker sees his own prop under pressure, grabs the opposition's leg, and the opposing flanker then whacks *him*, and bingo, trouble all round.

Derek: At senior level you've got your touch judges. Doing a school or junior game, you're on your own.

Ed: In some ways, it's more difficult to do a junior game than an international. You've got to work harder on some areas, educate people, teach them what's unacceptable before somebody else takes the law into his own hands. It's hard work.

Derek: And all the time they may be trying to con you.

Ed: Anybody who even contemplates that a side who wins the ball never collapses the scrum is living in Disneyland.

Derek: They'll always accuse each other.

Ed: Imagine the situation where you're one point ahead, or behind. A minute to go. Your put-in. What's the easiest thing? You drop the scrum on your own ball.

Derek: It's a gamble.

Ed: Odds are in your favour. Ten to one the referee will give a penalty against the other side. I saw a senior game recently where side A did not push side B one inch in the whole game. Several scrums collapsed, but nobody was penalised. Right at the end: a 5-metre scrum to side A. It was rock-solid, going nowhere. Then it collapsed – and the referee awarded Side A a penalty try! I can't understand how any referee could do that.

Derek: You reckon the average referee automatically suspects the non-winning side of collapsing.

Ed: Too many do. We've all got to think a bit harder. If your team's one point up, you're not likely to deliberately give away a penalty in front of your posts. If you're the attacking team, you might try to con the referee into guessing otherwise. Once a referee lets himself guess, he's no longer in control of the game. The players are in control of the game.

Ed: Unless all the front row players keep their heads up as they engage, there's a risk of collapse. Here, Whites are looking up. Their backs are arched and they're ready to shove. But Blacks are looking down at the ground and their backs are curved. When the pressure comes on, the Black scrum will go down. I wouldn't allow them to engage like this. Incidentally, the hookers could have a tighter grip. If they can't reach around the props, I like to see them get good fistfuls of jersey.

Derek: What about scrums elsewhere on the field? A team that's won the ball might still collapse it. They get a penalty, bang the ball into the corner, get the throw-in. They'll con you if they can.

Ed: Derek Bevan told me, 'Always remember one thing: the players aren't your friends. They don't give two hoots for your career or mine. They don't give a damn for your reputation. They're only interested in their own careers.' That's very true. If a front row can squeeze a bad decision out of the referee and win the game, they're happy!

Derek: I reckon any 3rd XV would be delirious if they thought they'd conned an international referee.

Ed: I've no doubt they'll succeed, too. Front rows are not so stupid as some people make out. In certain parts of the field they *will* collapse the scrum, if they think they can get a kick at goal. There are times when a team is shunting the opposition back – on their own ball – and the front rows will go down. Of course, there's a good chance the opposition did it – but I've also had situations where I penalised the side in possession. They say,

Ed: If you don't see it, you can't give it. That's a fundamental rule of refereeing. Unless you actually saw the try scored, you can't award it – and the same applies throughout the game. A referee should never guess. Once he starts making decisions based on what he thought happened, he's in big trouble.

'We'd never collapse the scrum on our own ball, ref!' And I just smile.

Derek: Bluff and double-bluff.

Ed: Exactly. Mind you, fatigue can also be a factor, especially at the top level. Late in the game, sometimes the players get tired and when the scrum engages they don't hit hard, they just flop in, everything's loose. It's even worse if one team's dominant. The opposition just hasn't got the strength to stay up.

Derek: But there's the other situation where you get a front-row player who is strong and bloody-minded and simply keeps collapsing the scrum. He won't listen, he won't learn. What next?

Ed: If you're convinced the guy's deliberately collapsing, and you've warned him and his captain, and he still goes on ruining the game, well, he's left you no option. He's got to go. He's in the Sin Bin.

Derek: Have you ever done it?

Ed: Sent off a prop for persistent collapsing? No, because I've never had to. Clive Norling sent off two props when they repeatedly collapsed. It solved the problem.

Derek: And word gets around, doesn't it? The front rows of other clubs know what to expect.

Ed: Ripples in a pond. One yellow card can go a long way. The problem's got to be solved. *How* we solve it is immaterial, but the game can't afford to have scrums collapsing all the time. It's not what rugby's about.

COLLAPSING – AND THE LAW OF THE LAND

Derek: And at another level, the referee can't afford to get the scrums wrong. He's got a responsibility under civil law . . .

Ed: The law of the land doesn't stop when you cross the touch line. The referee has a duty under the civil law as well as the rugby law to protect the players from injury. As referee he's been given power to control the game and if he fails, and someone's hurt because of that, he could be in trouble.

Derek: And the fact that the referee wasn't getting paid, he was doing the job for the love of the game – that's irrelevant.

Ed: The precedent was established in 1996, when an injured player sued a rugby referee, and the judge ruled that the referee 'failed to exercise reasonable care and skill' in preventing scrum collapses. That was a very important case. It was the first of its kind in Britain, and obviously the first successful court case against a rugby referee.

Derek: It made for very sobering reading, didn't it? The match was a Colts game, and the injured player was only 17. The judge stressed that his ruling didn't apply to senior rugby, which just underlines the fact that when you have authority over youngsters – anyone under 18 – the law requires you to be extra careful about their safety.

Ed: Correct. They're not adults, they can't be expected to have an adult's maturity and understanding, so they're more vulnerable. Usually the referee is an adult, and young players expect him to protect them. So does the law.

Derek: That case produced a lot of sympathy for rugby referees as a breed, didn't it? Some rugby writers said front-row players are behaving irresponsibly and leaving the referee to carry the can if it all goes wrong.

Ed: There's some truth in that. Prop forwards can be negative and destructive. But that doesn't mean the referee can dodge his responsibilities. I go back to what I said earlier: you've got to *manage* the scrum from the very start. The worse they play the harder you referee, until either they scrummage properly or you stop all scrummaging before someone gets hurt. You won't be popular, but you're not out there to make friends.

Derek: The safety of the player has always been the referee's top priority, but nowadays he's got to protect his own back, too.

Ed: You've got it in one. And it's not enough just to blow the whistle. If we don't *manage* the scrum, the players aren't the only ones who could suffer. This is doubly true at the junior level. Senior players usually know what they're about. Junior scrummaging must be closely managed by the referee. It's crucial.

The Tackle

Derek: Law 15, the tackle law, is one of the shortest in the book. Basically, what it says is, when a player is tackled, the tackler must immediately release him, get up and move away. The tackled player must immediately pass or release the ball and move away so that arriving players, on their feet, can play it. Is that a fair summary?

Ed: Pretty fair. There's more detail, but that's the essence.

Derek: So in theory, a tackle should begin and end almost instantly. It should never be a long stoppage. Play should re-start without delay.

Ed: That's the theory, yes.

Derek: But you know and I know that it doesn't always happen. Often the tackle acts like a kind of clot in the bloodstream: it stops the game in its tracks. So what's the problem?

Ed: The game's getting faster all the time. It's this all-round speed that has had such an impact on the tackle situation. Fitness levels have improved so much over the last few years. We've always had fast stand-offs and threequarters; now we've got props and locks who are very quick and agile. So we're getting more people arriving at the breakdown, and arriving faster, more dynamically. For the referee, this can be a headache.

Derek: A headache because the ball isn't released?

Ed: Either it's not released, or it's released and then killed, or something similar . . . In the 1995 World Cup, a record was kept of every penalty kick awarded, and why. Offences involving handling the ball on the ground or killing the ball accounted for a huge percentage – half as many *more* than all the line-out and scrum offences put together. My guess is that the bulk of those penalties followed tackles. In the game as a whole, there are more penalties given from the tackle or what follows it – a pile-up, or people going over the top – than any other part of the game.

Derek: So it follows that if only we could straighten out the tackle, we'd get more rugby.

Ed: The tackle needs to be coached better, played better and refereed better. There's been too much confusion about what we're trying to achieve. It's a part of the game we need to identify very clearly.

Derek: But the law defines it beautifully. What is it about the tackle that we don't get from the Lawbook?

Ed: The reality is that, as referees, in order to make the tackle law work, we're giving an element of sympathy to the ball-carrier, and to his team-mates.

Derek: Sympathy. Now there's a word you won't find in the laws.

Ed: There's a lot more to refereeing than reading the Lawbook.

Derek: Agreed. So tell me more about this sympathy.

Ed: Okay, let's look at the sequence of events. The ball-carrier is tackled, he goes to ground. We're trying to give him some *time* to do something *positive* with the ball. The law says releasing it can include putting it on the ground. Now he can't wait ten minutes, or even ten seconds, before he decides to release it. We're still looking for him to do something *quickly.* But we're trying to give him all the opportunities we can to actually do something positive with the ball. When he places it, as a referee I want to see him place it *away from his body.* The ball is visible to me, and that makes refereeing ten times easier.

IMMEDIATE RELEASE

Derek: Now, the Lawbook uses this terrible word 'immediately'.

Ed: Yes. 'Immediate' might mean different things to different

Ed: *This sequence shows three stages of the tackle. First, in (a), White tackles Black. Note that White not only has his arms around Black, he also has a hand on the ball. In (b), both players have released the ball – and the tackler has also released his opponent. This is what the law requires. It also requires both players to make the ball available. Once it's released, they must both move away from it or get up. And here, in (c), is the reward: a third player arrives and scoops up the ball. Play goes on. The tackle has interrupted the game but it hasn't stopped it – because both players have been positive in making continuous play possible.*

people. But what was agreed was that we would try to *improve* the game so the ball *comes away* from that tackle situation, so the ball's alive, so we don't end up with heaps of bodies around it and the referee having to blow his whistle anyway. To achieve this, we *are* giving the tackled player more opportunity to do something positive with the ball than possibly the law is telling us in black and white.

Derek: When the tackle law was changed, so that the tackled player could place the ball rather than just let go of it, that was what he did: he reached out, placed the ball, and left it there. But now that's developed into something different. He puts the ball on the ground and *he keeps his hand on it.* That's not releasing.

Ed: Well . . .

Derek: He's holding it steady for a team-mate to pick up.

Ed: Yes.

Derek: So there's release, and there's release. If he hugs the ball to his chest, we penalise him. If he places it and holds it, we don't.

Ed: All these tackle situations were thoroughly discussed, and it was fully agreed that the game would benefit if the ball wasn't just thrown away from a tackle, but actually placed and controlled. Coaches certainly argue that if the player leaves his hand there, there's more control over the ball.

Derek: Less likely the next bloke will knock it on.

Ed: Exactly. We're trying to do away with untidy situations around the tackle. We're looking for a tidy package. If the tackle goes to ground and the ball's controlled, it's much easier for the next player arriving – it could be *either* team – to actually get his hands on the ball. When it's bobbling about, the game becomes a mess. So this is just a way of *practically* refereeing the game.

Derek: Let's be clear about the tackle situation. It has no offside lines, does it? It's not like a ruck or maul.

Ed: True. What's special about the tackle zone is the way other players can join it, which is only through the Gate. I should say 'Gates' – one for each team. The Gate is as wide as the tackle zone. Any arriving player who wants to get involved must enter from behind that zone, through the Gate. 'Bums to posts,' as we say. Entry from the side is penalised. The only player this doesn't apply to is the tackler, because he's already in the zone.

Derek: I see. What else?

Ed: At a tackle, we want the next player who arrives to be on his feet. That's what the law says and it makes sense. Now, if you look at the pure physics of it, you're not always going to get a 17-stone guy running hard and reaching a tackle situation and stopping *dead*. It doesn't work like that. At one of the IRB's international collaborations they identified it as impossible. So what we said is this: You're allowed to step over the ball and take one step beyond. But that's where you stop. *Then* you can make contact with the opposition. If you go *past* that point and make contact, it becomes obstruction, because you're out in front of the ball.

Derek: The American football scenario.

Ed: That's it. I remember a game when I said to Norman Hadley, who weighs 18 stone, 'You're going too far past the ball.' And he

Ed: Here's the end of the tackle sequence – with a familiar bit of off-the-ball foul play. To protect his team-mate scooping up the ball, the large White player has over-run the scene of the tackle and knocked down a Black player, thus opening a channel for attack. The White player is, of course, guilty of Dangerous Play (for barging into an opponent without the ball). This aspect of American football is creeping (or charging) into rugby. We can't expect a big man to stop dead – but we can't allow him to keep going and flatten the opposition.

said to me, 'When a steam train gets going, it's very hard to stop.' Which is true. On the other hand, we can't afford to give these guys *carte blanche* to go however far *they want* past the ball.

Derek: If they can go too far, they will. They'll knock defenders over.

Ed: Of course they will. They'll clear a space ahead of the ball. That's why the international rugby community decided that they can step over the ball and take one step beyond – but no further.

Derek: Another thing: the tackler is not supposed to charge or barge the ball-carrier. Why don't you penalise this more often?

Ed: It's happening. I know where you're coming from on this. Long ago, Wales versus France in 1976, there was a famous occasion when J. P. R. Williams, full back, barged the French winger into touch, shoulder-to-shoulder. Last ditch stuff, very dramatic, totally illegal – the law says a tackler must grasp the ball-carrier with his arm or arms. No bulldozing. But as late as the 1991 World Cup, when I refereed Scotland versus Japan, Scott Hastings would have scored in the corner if this little Japanese guy hadn't bounced him into touch. It took great courage, it was pure theatre, and I didn't have it in my heart to penalise him. I mean, Scott was a big lad! But the law is very clear, and I'm sure that if the JPR thing happened today, he'd get penalised.

Derek: Because players' safety comes first?

Ed: Sometimes the tackler grabs and misses, then collides. Was that bad luck? It all comes down to the referee's judgement.

HIGH TACKLING

Derek: Does the same apply to high tackles? I mean, is it a high tackle when the ball-carrier *ducks* at the last moment?

Ed: Well . . . that's an interesting one, isn't it?

Derek: The tackler might be six foot four and the ball-carrier only four foot six.

Ed: With all types of foul play, the player's intent is what concerns me, and this applies especially to high tackles. Did he mean to tackle high? Or was it accidental? You have to decide instantly.

Ed: As a referee, 'intent' is a word I use a lot. Was it his *intent* to tackle high? Or was it caused by circumstances? You've got a split second to make your decision. I don't think the lawmakers were worried about guys who duck when they made that law. They were concerned about the player whose tackle *starts* high, who goes in *intending* to make a high tackle.

LATE TACKLING

Derek: Can you say the same thing about a late tackle? I'm thinking of the situation where a winger gets the ball, he knows an opponent is closing in on him, and he leaves his kick to the last possible instant. The tackler hits him a split second after the kick is made. Is that a late tackle? Or a late kick?

Ed: The criterion I try to use is this: if it's obvious to *me* that he's going to kick, then it should be obvious to the opposition. As usual, the referee has to be *reading* the game, all the time. If the guy with the ball delays, delays, delays, until his opponent is actually flying, is totally committed to the tackle, then it's very difficult for me to penalise. But if I can see that the player is going to chip over the top, and he does, and his opponent still comes thundering in, head down, then that's a late tackle. It all comes down to judgement. If the tackle coincides with the kick, I see nothing wrong with that.

Derek: Kickers do tempt fate sometimes.

Ed: Yes. And some guys try to buy a penalty, with swallow-dives and great roars of disapproval.

Derek: What do you watch? When you can see that a player is shaping to kick ahead, do you always keep an eye on him after he's kicked? The ball's in the air for a couple of seconds, you can afford to ignore it, briefly.

Ed: Before the match, I would have instructed my touch judges how we were going to handle this situation, and normally the nearest touch judge would follow the ball. I can't afford to linger, of course. I've got to be up with play – after all, a try might be scored, I need to be there. But . . . something inside you says: *I think this guy's going to come in late.* You read their body language, you just feel it. I'd like to think I'd be in a position to see the contact, and then just glance to see where the ball lands. And if I miss a late tackle, one of the touch judges should see it and flag. Then it's not enough just to whistle and say, 'Late tackle!' and award the penalty. We've got to make that player *know* that this sort of thing can't be allowed. Deal with the situation. Interestingly, everyone talks about the *late* tackle, but what's happening far more now is the *early* tackle.

Derek: A player gets tackled before he takes the pass?

Ed: Or when he's waiting to field a kick. That's more difficult, because you can get two guys in the air at the same time, a defender and an attacker. Is the attacker genuinely going for the ball, or is it an early tackle? Think how many teams put in a high kick to the full back . . .

Derek: If he's taken out by an early tackle, the defence is in big trouble.

Ed: Early tackling of a player waiting to catch a kick is a growing problem. The difference is often just a fraction of a second. I try to focus on the tackler's intent. When he has no idea where the ball is – like this player – then I reckon he's only interested in knocking his opponent down.

Ed: Exactly. We need to deal with that situation very quickly, tell the players, 'Whoa! You know the score. I don't want to see *that* again.'

Derek: Here's a thought. When the kicker gets late-tackled, his team has a choice: penalty kick either where the tackle happened or where the ball landed. Now, if a player gets early-tackled before he can catch a kick, why not give his team a similar choice? A penalty kick either where the early tackle happened or where the kick was made?

Ed: Well . . .

Derek: You say early tackles are a problem. This would discourage them.

Ed: Let me think about it.

Thud and Blunder

Derek: Here's the scenario. You're away from home. Straight from the kick-off, twenty-five blokes are fighting. What do you do?

Ed: I do the only thing I can: blow the whistle until they stop. But it's an awful position for any referee to be put in.

Derek: It gets worse. I forgot to tell you that this is only your second match as a referee.

Ed: What was my first match like?

Derek: Shambles.

Ed: I see . . . Still, I'm getting a lot of experience fast, aren't I? [LAUGHTER] Have they stopped fighting yet?

Derek: Yes. Now, the laws of the game are clear, but it's a very brave new referee who's going to say, 'Right! You're off, and you, and you . . .' After all, he doesn't see it happen on television.

Ed: It all comes down to commonsense and practicalities. What you want to do is identify the cause, isolate the guy responsible, and deal with him. If you can do that, everybody else becomes aware that if *they* perpetrate, the same thing will happen to them. It's much easier to use one person as an example. Of course you *can* warn every player in a punch-up – but if there's another punch-up, you send off both packs of forwards and everyone goes home.

Derek: It gets your name in the papers, but . . .

Ed: You become a martyr, and you probably won't be refereeing next week. Having said all that, it's still true that a player *can* be sent off in the first minute, and several have been, even at the highest level.

Derek: Obviously without a warning.

Ed: Certainly.

Derek: Thuggery is thuggery.

Ed: If a player does something brutal – deliberately kicks an opponent on the ground, for instance – and the referee doesn't send him off, that referee's lost control and credibility. And everyone else knows it. And the players are likely to think, 'Well, *we'd* better take charge, because *he* doesn't want to.' And that's a formula for disaster. But the reality is, most fights aren't as bad as that. Rugby players don't know how to box. Half the time they swing a punch and fall over.

Derek: Handbags at ten paces.

Ed: Yes. So, even when the players are doing their Rambo imitations, I try to keep a sense of proportion. There are three things that matter to me. One is the cause. Normally something happened to make someone react. What was it? If I can identify the perpetrator, that's good. Another is stopping the fight as quickly as possible. And the third is looking out for late arrivals – players who come flying in from far away and make the problem worse.

Derek: Okay. Now you know how to do it, because you've been there. Give some tips to the grassroots referee with a brand new whistle.

Ed: Don't get too close. If I'm next to a fight when it starts, I immediately back away. It's very easy to get caught up and mangled, and I'm not a particularly big person. I definitely never go in and start pulling players apart. I get concerned about referees who – with the best intentions – intervene in a fight and manhandle players.

Derek: I suppose they're afraid someone might get hurt.

Ed: The risk is, the referee might get hurt too. If you pull someone from behind, their instinct is to turn around and take a swing at you. I believe the only time it's safe to touch a player is when you shake hands with the captain before the match.

Derek: If you stand back, you get a better view of the fight.

Ed: That's right. So I'm watching, and I'm blowing the whistle as hard as I can, and I keep blowing unless it becomes obvious that these guys aren't taking any notice. Usually there's a couple of threequarters who have the sense to get out and stay out. That helps to isolate the actual scrap.

Derek: Do you say anything?

Ed: I do. I'm shouting all the time. Often there are some players shouting too – 'Get out!' or 'Don't get involved' – that sort of thing. Which helps.

Derek: While you're doing this, are you also saying to yourself, for instance, *Blue number 6 just thumped Red number 2?*

Ed: Exactly. I try to implant it on my memory. It's all part of working out what *caused* the eruption. Often it's all over quite quickly, because fighting is actually very exhausting, especially when guys are flinging great haymakers which *miss*. You can sometimes see them looking for someone to come in and stop them! They've had enough!

Derek: But they don't like to be seen to be backing off?

Ed: Well, they can't, can they? Not forwards. It's bad for the macho image. Now, if you've got a few people fighting and they're isolated, that's not a big problem for the referee. No matter how hard they're hitting each other, the referee can deal with it in a quite straightforward way. The big problem arises when outsiders rush in from a long way off, and get involved. The thing I find hideous is when guys run from the wing – 40 or 50 yards – and just plough in. The fight's nothing to do with them! Their job is to keep their shorts clean. So I stand well back and look out. I want to see who first caused the problem, and who made it worse.

Derek: South Africa versus Canada in the '95 World Cup.

Ed: If you look at the video of that incident, it all began with a tackle into touch by the opposing wingers. They had a disagreement, nothing special, and they were just beginning to relax their grip on one another when the other players came flying in. That was the real eruption, not the bit of wrestling by the wingers. Both teams were guilty, but one Canadian ran a *very* long way to get his punch in. When that happens it makes rugby look foolish. It's not a game for hooligans and it can't be allowed to become one. Having said that, I'm convinced the game is *cleaner* now than it's ever been. When I think of senior club games I used to watch a few years ago, before we had the Team of Three . . . Dear oh dear. Some nasty incidents. The players are more responsible nowadays. The clubs have weeded out all the psychopaths. Well, nearly all.

COOLING THE PLAYERS DOWN

Derek: Now then: the fight ends. The fists stop swinging. Let's assume nobody's hurt. What do you do next?

Ed: What I do is very slow and deliberate. Some might say laborious. I tell both teams to separate and retire. I get them 15 or 20 metres away from each other. They may not want to back off, but I persist until they've done it. Then I go over to my touch judge – assuming this is a senior game – but I never turn my back on the players, in case the trouble flares up again. If it does and I can catch the guy who does it, I'll use him as an example to the others, which is useful. So I go to the touch judge, even if he hasn't flagged for foul play, and I ask him what he saw. All the time I'm looking infield, at the players. They know what's happening. It makes them *think*. Makes them cool down. Now, if I've seen who started the fight or if the touch judge has seen, and if either of us can identify foul play, I have something to work on. I can begin to solve the problem.

Derek: That doesn't always happen, though, does it? The ball leaves a maul and gets shuttled across-field. As you follow it, a monumental punch-up breaks out behind you. You saw nothing of the cause. The touch judge saw nothing – his view was obscured. *Now* what do you do?

Ed: I call the two captains together. I say something like: 'You've got twenty seconds to talk to your players. If you can't control them, if you can't get them to behave in a proper manner, then we're going to have a problem.' You see: the referee cannot carry the entire burden of the game. Not only *cannot*. He *should not*. It's the players' responsibility to discipline themselves and play with self-control. If you put all that responsibility onto the referee's shoulders you'll just crush him.

Derek: And the game won't work.

Ed: It can't work, not like that. It's up to the players to take their share of responsibility. And the captains have a *massive* role to play. If the captain is a man of worth, he'll have the authority to instil some discipline into his team. So the referee must use him. Otherwise the referee will be struggling with a task that really shouldn't be his in the first place.

Derek: You've talked to the touch judge and the captains. Nobody gets sent off. How do you re-start play?

Ed: If the situation was serious enough, and I wanted to use time as a healer, I would probably penalise somebody. This isn't guesswork. Both sides have been fighting, both sides are guilty of foul play. The interesting point is: who do you penalise? If they're both equally guilty, you don't want to give a penalty that lets one team kick a goal: you've given them a crazy advantage if you do. My instinct would be to penalise the *attacking* team, the team in their opponents' half.

Derek: Preferably deep in their half.

Ed: And let the defending side kick out. That gives me a few seconds while they get to the line-out, and then a few more seconds while the line-out's being formed. Plus I'll be a bit fussy about this, so as to make my presence felt. And I'm just killing time, hoping the perpetrators will cool down, get the message and start behaving accordingly. It takes time to forget. I want them to forget.

Derek: Right. They forget, but soon they remember again and there's more trouble, only worse. Now what?

Ed: *After the brawl, separate the factions. It's essential to get the teams well apart, at least ten or fifteen yards. Never turn your back on the players, even when you're consulting your touch judge. Then take the perpetrator and his captain well away from both teams, so that everybody can see what's happening and nobody can interfere. Stay calm. The worse the problem, the calmer the referee must be. You can be calm and forceful at the same time.*

Ed: Well, you're running out of options, aren't you? If I can identify the troublemaker, I'll give him a serious talking-to.

Derek: It's a bit of a ceremony, that, isn't it? The referee moves into a wide open space and calls the offender to him. What's the object of the exercise?

Ed: It's to isolate the guy and make him clearly identifiable, so that everybody watching knows who the referee has picked out as the perpetrator. If I just stand in a huddle of players and talk, I'm not sending much of a message. But if I pull him out, and his captain too, that's different. It tells them I'm in control. I don't go in for a big showdown – I'm not trying to belittle the guy – I just talk quietly, say what's acceptable and unacceptable. And all the time, the other players' eyes are on you. Even if *he* isn't getting the message, maybe the others are!

ABSORBING THE FLAK

Derek: Not many outbreaks of violence are totally the fault of one side, are they? There's often a degree of provocation. Someone bit him in the leg, and he reacted, and now he's penalised for it. Your little lecture may make him even angrier.

Ed: That's why the referee must always be calm. Ultra-calm. It's no good being hostile or challenging to someone who's already feeling aggressive. When two aggressive people come together, that's a formula for disaster. The only way to calm someone aggressive is to be utterly calm yourself. No matter how much flak is coming your way, you've got to be able to take it and absorb it and carry on in the same calm, assured way. The more fraught the situation, the calmer the referee must appear to be. The person who wins the argument is always the guy who's calm and in control of himself, not the guy who's boiling over with aggression.

Derek: Now, being calm – is that the same as never being angry?

Ed: No. Sometimes you can call a player over, and without raising your voice, just by your manner and your general attitude, you can make it clear that you're very angry at what he's done.

Derek: Is this a matter of body English? As much as words?

Ed: Oh, it's *more* body English than words. And with me having a bit of a reputation of being a sort of 'players' referee', his team-mates will pick up the vibes and say, 'Hey, he's really pissed-off . . .' And if I'm as angry as that, I'll tell the captain: 'D'you realise this guy's just upset me?' Still very calm, very controlled. 'If *that's* how you want to play it, we can play it that way.' Putting the onus on the captain to straighten out his player. And when they go away you can often hear him doing just that. But you mustn't let your feelings interfere with the nuts-and-bolts routine of your job. I got so angry in one particular senior game that I made a mistake.

There was a maul, and I saw a guy grab the ball-carrier's leg and drag it back in order to collapse the maul. That was such a colossal piece of stupidity – he could easily have broken his leg – that I was furious. Everyone knew it. I didn't shout, I was quiet and controlled, but the body-English told everyone that I was shocked by such a dangerous foul. The trouble was, I was so furious that I forgot to use the card. Unforgivable.

CARDS AND CAUTIONS

Derek: Yellow and red cards. What difference have they made to the game?

Ed: A lot. They've given the referee an extra sanction. A bit of muscle he can use to stop the game going haywire. There's no doubt that, before we had cards, referees were often reluctant to send off someone whose play wasn't dangerous but it was ruining the game.

Derek: Down to 14, a team's in real trouble.

Ed: And the referee may have decided the result. But when he Sin-Bins a player, say a flanker who's repeatedly off-side at mauls, that team is a man short for only ten minutes' playing time. It's a middle way between a penalty kick and a sending off, and it sends a message to everyone else: this referee means business. The captains know, because I always caution or card a player in front of his captain. The captain's a witness. For a card I note the player's name too.

Derek: That's fine if you can identify the individual. But half the team might be to blame. What then? General warning?

Ed: Be careful. General warnings are dangerous things. You can only do it once, and you'd better be ready to back it up. Otherwise you're in an even worse position. And you'd better be clear about exactly what you mean by 'general'. I remember when I refereed Romania versus France, there was more and more niggle between the forwards. It got steadily worse. After 20 minutes I called the captains together and said, 'This is a general warning for numbers 1 to 8 on both teams. From now on, if any one of your forwards causes any trouble, he will leave the field-of-play. Do you understand?' They understood, and all went well until ten minutes from the end when somebody kicked somebody and he had to leave. Now, if I'd said, 'Right – this is a general warning for the whole team,' and five minutes later the poor old winger (who's been as good as gold so far) commits a late tackle – he's got to go. I've always had difficulty in accepting that. It seems very harsh. A general warning is the big trump card, and you really have to be very careful how you play it.

Ed: Showing the yellow (or red) card is not a dramatic performance. Don't wave it about. The players are watching – they'll know as soon as they see it. Just show it. That's enough to get the message across.

Derek: Let's suppose you're left with no choice and you send two blokes off. What do you write down?

Ed: The time, the player's name – first name and last name – and his number. And I'd make a mental note of the details of what he'd done, but I wouldn't necessarily write that down. At senior level I tell my touch judges to record cautions and sendings-off as well. And before the match I not only check the programme, I also ask if there have been any last-minute changes. At senior level I probably know who the player is anyway, but if I have to send him off I always ask his name. It's too important to risk a mistake.

Derek: Also, you'll need his name for your report.

Ed: Certainly. And reports to disciplinary committees are very important. Some are terrible – badly written, incomplete, confusing. I think referees need guidance and training in how to write those reports.

Derek: Sure. Otherwise the disciplinary committee can't do its job, can it? There was a case recently where the report was such a mess that the committee couldn't understand a word of it. They were ready to acquit the guy. Then the referee arrived, the committee questioned him, got the facts, and suspended the player for 144 days!

Ed: The report should be simple, straightforward, above all *factual*. State the playing conditions, tempo of the game, then say, for instance: 'In the 30th minute of the first half, Red left wing, Bill Bloggs, kicked an opponent on the ground, 10 metres from the ball. I sent him off, under Law 10.4.' No guesswork. Just the facts.

Derek: That's always assuming his real name is Bloggs.

Ed: Ah, well. You hear of it happening a lot in amateur soccer: players giving false names. But if it happens to me in rugby, as a referee there's nothing I can do about it. I always tell referees: don't get embroiled in the disciplinary process. Don't get upset if you feel that a disciplinary committee has not supported you. The only thing that matters is *you* have seen something that merited a sending-off, and you've sent the player off. You've done what *you* felt was right. Now it's up to the judge and jury to decide how long he gets. It's not your job. Put it out of your mind. You've got enough problems already. Of course, if the player gives you an obviously false name, you would question it. If they insist that it is his name, and you know it's not, that's something else to go in your report. Let the Union involved deal with it.

Derek: Very wise. There are people who have changed their name to Elvis Presley. I mean, legally.

Ed: There you go, then.

WHODUNNIT?

Derek: One last scenario. This is the kind of really tough decision you're unlikely to have to make in an international match, but it happened to me in a very junior 2nd XV game. In open play, a long way from the ball, a player got kicked when he was on the ground. Kicked *hard*. I saw none of it. Half the players did. They thumped the villain, his team-mates retaliated, there was quite a little battle. Very, very nasty. Someone could have been badly hurt. What's the answer?

Ed: Long term, clubs shouldn't have players who kick opponents! That's where the responsibility lies: with the clubs, and they can't be allowed to put it onto the referee. Short-term . . . If the referee thinks the incident is serious enough he should report it and let the Union investigate. But in the match, he cannot send a player off for something he didn't see. Now, I've been in a situation like this, where players have been injured, obviously through foul play, and neither I nor the touch judges have seen it. That's when I've used the captains. I stopped the game and told them: 'Something's obviously happened. I haven't seen it. Let's make it absolutely clear: I'm going to be looking even harder from now on, and if I see *anybody* guilty of foul play of *any* kind, they will be dismissed immediately. Do you understand that? You know where I'm coming from?'

Derek: The difficulty is, they know something you don't know. They know whodunnit.

Ed: Well, I don't stop there. It's very important for me to speak to the victim *and* his captain, and say, 'Look, you've got to let *me* deal with this. Don't take the law into your own hands.' Because if that player retaliates and whacks the guy who fouled him, you might have to send him off, and that's not a happy ending. So talk to the team that's suffered. Say: 'Look, lads: I've missed it, you know that. You know who did it. Now don't make it worse.' You can even ask them who they think did it. Never believe everything they say. Just have it in the back of your mind.

Derek: A lot of referees would give a rocket to the team they believed guilty and get on with the game.

Ed: That's not enough. Everything comes back to the players feeling confident in you, being comfortable with what you're trying to do. You've got to *work* to get their confidence. And that means working on both teams.

'Back Ten!'

Derek: Soccer players envy our power to send players back ten metres for backchat, or slow retreat, or whatever. 'If only we had your *Back Ten*,' they say.

Ed: I very rarely use it.

Derek: You amaze me.

Ed: Very often when we send people back ten, we've not solved the problem that caused the penalty in the first place. And refereeing is all about solving problems. That's *exactly* what you're doing. Problems arise; you manage them; you solve them. Now, 'Back ten'! is a lovely little weapon to have in your armoury, but it doesn't solve the initial problem, does it? Sometimes it can make that problem worse. Certainly when you're playing international rugby, the French and the Italians find it difficult to come to terms with 'Back ten, back ten!' It doesn't fit easily into their culture. If you do it to them *initially*, without attempting to solve the problem, you're going to be marching them back ten all day. And the problem won't have gone away, probably.

Derek: Okay, let's pick a problem. Suppose it's just straightforward old-fashioned dissent. You give a penalty kick for, say, not releasing the ball after a tackle. Another player, ten metres away, says, 'Oh, I never heard such crap in all my life!' Now – do you march that team back ten, or . . .

Ed: No, I don't. The moment you let someone shout comments like that, your authority is totally undermined. So I think: *Hang on a minute, we've got a serious case of dissent here. Knocking them back ten is not enough.* I stop the game, call the guy and his captain over, because this is an ideal opportunity for the referee to show his authority. Not to throw his weight about; quite the opposite. I say, quietly, 'There's one thing we'd better understand here. *That* level of behaviour is unacceptable. If *you* do it again, you're gone.' And I tell the captain, 'If any of your players do it, maybe *they* might go as well. Captain – get hold of them, get control of them.' That works for me.

Derek: Why say 'they *might* go'? Why not say 'they will definitely go'?

Ed: Because that totally commits you. It's better to leave yourself some room for manoeuvre.

Derek: Suppose you didn't call the guy over and so on. Suppose you knocked them back ten and the opposition kicked the penalty goal. Isn't there a message in that too? Dissent cost his team three points. He won't forget that in a hurry.

Ed: Maybe. Maybe not. Some players don't think that way. Some players don't think *at all*; you have to tell them what to think. And what if the opposition misses the kick at goal? The guy's got away with calling your decision crap. But in any case – whether the kick is good or not – *you*, the referee, have *lost* some authority. That means, inevitably, the player's confidence in you is diminished. Whereas if you call the guy out and tell his captain, 'It's *your* problem – you sort him out, or I'll have to deal with it, and that means he disappears', then the level of confidence you need from both teams will be raised.

Derek: All right: no 'back ten' in that case. So when *would* you march a team back ten?

Ed: Well, if I penalise them and they deliberately don't go back ten from the original penalty kick . . . But if my first 'back ten' didn't succeed, I wouldn't persist in knocking them back again and again, because – you've heard this before – *that's not solving the problem*. I need to stop the game and say, 'Now, Captain! Come here, please. Me and you have got a problem. Your guys are not attempting to retire. You're stopping this team from gaining any advantage from the penalty. Now, either you sort it out – or we're both going to have a much bigger problem.' You see, shouting 'Back ten, back ten, back ten' all day – that's not a game of rugby. The situation needs to be *managed*, so as to make the game possible.

SHOWDOWN IN BRISBANE

Derek: Now, there was one international match where presumably you ran out of options and the man had to go.

Ed: Yes. James Small, the Springbok winger.

Derek: Australia versus South Africa, 1994, in Brisbane.

Ed: It was an unusual incident. It's unusual for a winger to get sent off, and it's unusual for *anyone* to get sent off for dissent. James Small had already been involved in a few incidents on that tour. He'd become the guy the crowd loved to hate, and at Brisbane they were really giving him some stick – Brisbane is a relatively small ground and the spectators are very close to the field.

Derek: The Aussies can be quite outspoken, I believe.

Ed: That's one word for it. So James was getting all this flak, and he wasn't getting much ball, and finally he got totally frustrated and he just boiled over. Ten minutes from the end of the match he lost his cool entirely and said something that was unacceptable.

Derek: Directly to you?

Ed: Yes. He didn't agree when I awarded a penalty against his team. So that was dissent.

Derek: And what he said was . . .

Ed: Well, I can't repeat it, because I'm sworn to secrecy, but . . .

Derek: But it was pretty ripe? Addressed to you?

Ed: Yes. I very rarely lose my temper, and a friend who saw it all on television said my eyes changed suddenly and quite . . . dramatically. That's something I try to avoid. I think it's imperative that referees appear always calm and assured. But on this occasion my body language should have told the players that I was very angry. Remember that James Small, being on the wing, was some distance away. I said to him, 'I suggest you put your hands in your pockets and go back ten.'

Derek: And he did?

Ed: Yes. He went back ten, but then he repeated what he'd said before. And I sent him off.

Derek: Let's be absolutely clear: his language was bad?

Ed: Oh yes. He had to go. I've met him many times since then, including the World Cup Final, and there's no friction – we've wished each other well. But on reflection, I think we each learned something from that incident. There's no doubt he was a problem on the Australian tour. Short-fused. After the sending-off he began to mature, so maybe it helped his career. As for me: I would probably handle that situation differently now. You see, when I sent him back ten, I didn't solve the problem.

Derek: Because you didn't relate him personally to the 'back ten'? Because he was so far away?

Ed: Exactly. What I would probably do now is stop the game, call him over the first time he used that language, and speak to him, maybe even caution him.

Derek: In which case he probably would never repeat it.

Ed: And we might not end up with a sending-off. Although, to be honest, his first comment warranted a sending-off.

WHERE'S THE SKIPPER?

Derek: Now, what you said earlier about using the captain is all very well if you're at Twickenham or Ellis Park or Brisbane, but what if you're refereeing some hairy 3rd XV on a remote, windswept park pitch, and the regular captain broke his leg last week, so this is the first time ever that this new chap has captained a side – does your approach still work?

Ed: It's got to work. Refereeing can be very difficult at a lower level of rugby – I know, because I've been there, I've done it. But even at that level, if players aren't going back ten when you penalise, you've got to ask the question: why aren't they? Ask the captain: 'You know you should be retiring. Can you tell me why you're not?' If he says, 'Because we don't want to', you say, 'Right! I'll tell you something. From now on, you *will* go back ten.' And you get to work, *managing* that situation, *solving* that problem. If you have to force a team back ten from the first minute to the last, you haven't solved the problem.

Derek: Suppose the captain says – and it's been said to me – 'They won't pay any attention to me, ref.'

Ed: Well, then you've got to pick on some player and make an example of him. Apply the law of repeated infringement, caution him, do *something*, find a way to make them change their attitude. Solving problems is not always easy. You can't always tell the captain to do it. You've got to search for ways of managing and solving, and these differ from game to game, depending on the circumstances. A referee who is confident, and who inspires confidence, can solve any problems thrown in front of him. *Any* problems. If he's lacking in confidence, then he's going to find it hard going, and the whistle alone won't save him. Players don't respect the whistle. They respect the man.

Derek: Back to captains. Are you happier with a captain who is close at hand?

Ed: I don't like wingers or fullbacks as captains. I do like forwards or scrum-halves. They're making the big decisions, and it helps when we see a lot of each other. It must have been difficult for Ieuan Evans, on the wing. When I refereed Wales and Euan was captain, messages were always being shuttled back and forth. Sometimes he ran in and I met him halfway. Not easy. But the captain's role is crucially important. My feeling is we've never taken it seriously in this country. We've elected the best looking guy, or . . .

Derek: Or the tallest.

Ed: Yes, or the best player.

Derek: Who isn't necessarily the best leader.

Ed: What we should be saying is, 'This guy can *control* these players. He's a good decision-maker. Make *him* captain.' What's more, I think it's only right and proper that we, as referees, should expect him to fulfil that role. If there's a problem, he should want to know what's causing it and how to resolve it. Sean Fitzpatrick is probably the best captain I've met in that respect. He was very, very good. But in general the game hasn't made the most of captains. I'd like to see the Unions offer them some professional training. Help them become better decision-makers and problem-solvers. They need it.

Derek: Certainly, the further you go down the game, the less influence the captain has.

Ed: Yes. But at any level, rugby players are rugby players. Point them in the right direction and they'll respond.

Repeated Infringement

Derek: If there's one law of the game that most players don't understand – in fact many have never heard of it – it's Repeated Infringement.

Ed: And it's part of the Foul Play Law, so the consequences could be serious. Mind you, I don't suppose I knew anything about it, when I was playing.

Derek: What the law actually says is that a player who repeatedly infringes *any* law – not just the heavy stuff – must be cautioned and Sin-Binned. Whether or not he *meant* to infringe is beside the point. He kept doing it, so he's got to go.

Ed: And being Sin-Binned doesn't wipe his slate clean. If he comes back and infringes in the same way again, or if he commits any other offence that's cautionable – well, Good-night Vienna. Second yellow means an automatic red. He's gone for good.

Derek: Powerful medicine.

Ed: And not always easy to apply because, as a referee, you haven't always got time to think: 'That guy's done that before!' But it's being penalised more and more, now that the game has entered this entertainment mode, because when we've got a guy who's actually spoiling the afternoon, he must be dealt with. Otherwise the problem only grows. Bear in mind the law lets the referee relax his standard in junior matches. Poor skills might be to blame there.

Derek: Where does Repeated Infringement most affect the game?

PENALTY TRY

Ed: Mainly offside and killing the ball on the ground. The thinking is: 'We'll give away three points instead of five.' I mean, that was obviously the case in the 1995 Varsity match.

Derek: Time running out, Oxford leading by more than three points, Cambridge battering away at the Oxford line.

Ed: And Tony Spreadbury awarded a penalty try against Oxford.

Derek: For which he took a lot of stick from some rugby writers.

Ed: Some. Not all. These rugby writers are quite funny fellows, aren't they? Some of them feel they know the laws inside-out, and on the day they turn out to be not quite so correct as they thought they were, whereas others really take the trouble to know their stuff and get it right. They know Law 9 says a try shall be awarded if one would probably have been scored but for foul play by the opposing team, and they know that Law 10 says repeated infringement is foul play. The problem in the Varsity match was that Oxford were repeatedly offside a couple of metres from their line.

Derek: Let's identify the actual sequence of events. Tony penalised Oxford, but the penalty kick was always on the 5-metre line, because that's the nearest to the goal line that a team is allowed to take a penalty.

Ed: And Cambridge needed a try, so they always took a tap-kick and went for the line. But Oxford never retired to their goal line, as the law requires. They stayed in the 5-metre gap and blocked the Cambridge attack. They were repeatedly offside. Tony decided – and he's closer to the action than anyone else – that Oxford were *deliberately* conceding penalties. There's no more professional foul than that. Tony punished Oxford with a penalty try, and I think that it was a brave and correct decision.

THE TEAM IS THE OFFENDER

Derek: Perhaps the reason why some people objected to it was that they had always associated the penalty try with a single offence by a single player. Tripping the winger, for example.

Ed: That's probably so. But the law makes it very clear that if the referee decides that *different* players are committing the *same* offence, then that adds up to repeated infringement by that team and the referee should give a general warning. Knowing Tony, I'm sure he spoke up. Tony's a very vocal referee. The plain truth is that Oxford would have continued giving away penalties for offside all afternoon, to stop Cambridge scoring, and that's not what our game is about. Same applied at the 1996 Pilkington Cup Final, where Leicester conceded a string of penalties to keep Bath out and Steve Lander awarded a penalty try.

Derek: But if it's so obvious, why was there such a howl of wrath?

Ed: I think there has been a weakness in refereeing. All of us have not done what Tony did, in certain circumstances. And to be honest, awarding a penalty try is something that's not natural for me; in fact, I find it very unnatural. But I took a game – it was Neath versus Fiji – where the Fiji No. 2 came over the top of a ruck and killed the ball, *twice* in succession. This was very near the Fiji goal line. Neath wanted to take a quick penalty. I stopped them, called the Fiji player over and said: 'If you do that again you could be sent off. At the same time you could concede a penalty try.' It was one of those flashpoint situations: if I hadn't blown up very quickly, Neath would have sorted him out with their feet.

Derek: Rucked him out with the ball, as the All Blacks do.

Ed: He was a New Zealander, as it happened, and he took what was coming to him without flinching . . . But that's not the main issue. Looking back on that game, I think I would have been well within my rights to give a penalty try. The Fijians would have considered it very harsh, but it would have made a point. Maybe as referees we've not been good enough at making the point to players that repeated offences are not acceptable. They ruin the afternoon!

Derek: It's tough on the referee, isn't it? Yet another big decision on his shoulders. Seven points could turn a game.

BEWARE THE BANANA

Ed: It's not easy. But the referee should never concern himself with the result. Who wins and who loses shouldn't interfere with his job, which is simply to apply the laws. I suppose the ideal solution is to catch a guy early, so you can *use* him as an example to others, without having to bring out your heavy artillery. Take the Sale versus Northampton game I refereed. When Sale were defending, their winger was repeatedly offside. He was two yards up. This banana-shaped line is no accident; it's something they practise in training – senior players have told me so. If their opponents get possession, there's no way they'll move the ball to *their* winger.

Derek: He'd get man and ball together.

Ed: The ball's never even going to arrive. That option is closed down. Part of the game is killed. Another penalty, another stoppage, another problem. So I spoke to Sale's captain, Paul Turner. 'If he does it again, he's off,' I said. 'You're his captain – you tell him.' Paul was a smart and experienced player. The problem stopped, and I didn't have to distort the game by sending someone off. By the way, that winger's not playing for Sale any more!

[LAUGHTER]

Derek: Teams don't like it when you give them a penalty and stop the game to have words with the opposition.

Ed: Tough luck. One of the drawbacks of the modern game is the lack of breaks. The quick penalty and free kick have opened up the game superbly but they've also destroyed opportunities for us to manage situations. From time to time we may have to *stop* the game – tell the team *not* to take the kick – in order to buy some time and *manage* a situation before it turns sour and we end up sending someone off or giving penalty tries.

Derek: Going back to the Varsity Match episode: when an attacking team takes a quick tapped penalty on the 5-metre line, the goal line is the defenders' offside line and so they've got to get behind it – which means they're running in the same direction as the ball-carrier. His chances of scoring should be pretty good.

Ed: And that's not all. There's a cute little ploy being used at penalty or free kicks. The team takes a tap-kick and runs directly at and into the opponent in front. They're trying to buy another ten metres, and if the kick's near the opposition goal line, they may be trying to buy a penalty try too! So, as a referee, you've got to make your mind up very quickly. Was the defender making an effort to retire? If he was, and an attacker ran into him . . .

Derek: That just shows one guy was running faster than the other.

Ed: Exactly. And the attacker will argue that the defender was just making himself awkward, that he shouldn't have been in that space anyway! It's a difficult decision. We're going to see more penalty tries: that's my feeling. The IRB are saying, 'Look, the law's there, let's start using it.' Well, if a team deserves to concede a penalty try, that's no problem. But it's not an *alternative* to managing the game and trying to achieve fair play by other means. A penalty try is almost our last resort. Let's not devalue it through over-use.

The 3-Game Scenario

Derek: I've heard you say that the game can be won or lost – as far as the referee's concerned – before the toss-up.

Ed: That's right.

Derek: That's going to surprise a few people.

Ed: Well, I've seen it happen. Many times.

Derek: You're saying that the referee can throw it all away before the ball's even been kicked? He's missed a trick somewhere. What's gone wrong?

Ed: It all comes down to the 3-Game Scenario: the game before, during and after. Each is vital. How you behave before the match is just as important as how you behave during the eighty minutes; and what you do after the match will affect your performance in future games.

Derek: What you're telling me is there's far more to refereeing than just refereeing?

Ed: Correct. And I'm not talking about fitness training or diet, although they're both important. I'm talking about the ability of the individual to *manage* a situation, to his own advantage. It's a complex matter, but the best shorthand description I know is the 'feel-good factor', and it comes from confidence. Your confidence in them and their confidence in you. And I'm absolutely convinced that the players either *will* or *will not* have confidence in you before you even step onto the pitch. If they haven't got it – you're lost. This pre-match element has never been given the importance it deserves in the training of referees, in my opinion.

THE GAME 'BEFORE'

Derek: Okay. Stop there. Everything you've said so far is theory. How does it work in practice? Give us the nuts-and-bolts.

Ed: All right. For instance . . . Look, I'll give you a bad example. Or rather, a good example of a bad way to behave. This actually happened before the 2nd XV game of a junior club. The referee strode into the dressing-room and announced: 'I want to check the studs.' 'No problem,' the captain said. 'I also want to check their fingernails,' the referee said. Everyone laughed. 'I'm not joking,' he said. They all held their hands out. One guy said, 'I'm sorry they're dirty. I've come straight from work.' The referee said, 'Any more cheek from you and I'll start the game with a penalty.'

Derek: And he still wasn't joking?

Ed: Deadly serious. The guys looked at each other and thought: *Oh God . . . we're in for one of those afternoons . . .* And that's exactly how it turned out. A miserable afternoon for all thirty players and the spectators. And the referee couldn't have enjoyed it, either.

Derek: He'd blown it.

Ed: He never had a chance before they started. In the 3-Game Scenario, his game 'before' had ruined his game 'during'. And it probably hadn't done his *next* game any good.

Derek: How do you explain his behaviour? Bad egg for breakfast? Power complex? Inexperience?

Ed: Actually, he was quite an experienced ref. What had happened was, in his game the week before, someone had got gouged – at least, he thought so.

Derek: Ah. So now he's obsessed with fingernails.

Ed: His motives were good.

Derek: His methods were lousy.

Ed: What he *could* have done, he could have said to the captain, 'Last week I had a nasty incident with fingernails. Could you ask your players to check theirs, in case they're a bit long . . .' They would have thought well of him for that. It's how you approach things that matters.

Derek: Well, given that fingernails are not a common problem, what else matters?

Ed: Everything matters.

Derek: What do you mean?

Ed: I mean that from the minute the referee arrives at the ground, he's being judged. Everything he does makes an impression, good or bad. If he turns up late, they think he may be sloppy or ill-organised. If he seems rushed and anxious, that's not a very encouraging sign, either. I like to get to the ground at least an hour before the kick-off. Have a cup of tea and walk around. There's always someone to chat to. If you lock yourself away in the ref's room and do the crossword, people might think you don't like them; whereas if you make yourself available . . .

Derek: And who knows? You might learn something.

Ed: Especially if you've been sent to a different part of the country and you don't know the clubs. I remember, many years ago, going to referee in the Forest of Dean, which as we all know is a hotbed of rugby.

Derek: They certainly take it very seriously.

Ed: Cinderford were at home to Lydney, under floodlights. Cinderford brass band was playing on the pitch, both mayors were present, it looked like a wonderful little event! From the kick-off, there was the biggest brawl I'd ever seen. I think five guys were *not* fighting. I found out afterwards that the fixture had been abandoned fifteen years earlier, because of . . . well, sheer hatred. And this match was supposed to bring the clubs together again!

Derek: Nobody told the players.

Ed: Nobody told the referee! Now, if I'd done a bit of homework, asked a few little subtle questions – how are the clubs doing? where are they in the league? what happened the last time they met? – I might have been forewarned and forearmed.

Derek: While you're doing your homework on them, is it possible that they have already done their homework on you?

Ed: Oh, certainly. At the senior level, if the coaches don't already know a referee, they'll find out his strengths and weaknesses. Without a doubt.

Derek: Does this mean that part of the 'game before the game' is going to be a session with the coaches and captains?

Ed: Possibly. But I never approach *them*, other than for the toss-up and so on. I never call them in for any pre-match conference about how the game's going to be handled. Never. Now, if a coach or captain has a question about an interpretation of a certain law, I'm more than happy to speak to him – because any problem we can sort out before the game is one less problem for me to solve during the eighty minutes. But to be honest, the last thing I want before a match is a long discussion. You do meet these great enthusiasts – not players – who want to pick your brains about all the finer points of law. I usually make an excuse and say I've got to inspect the pitch!

YOU'RE BEING JUDGED

Derek: Now, according to your 3-Game Scenario, the teams have already begun to judge you.

Ed: That's inevitable. As soon as they see you, they start to form an opinion. Very ordinary things can be very important. Have you shaved properly? Is that a soup-stain on your tie? Why don't you smile? Whether you like it or not, players are going to react to your appearance. If you look gloomy, maybe they'll think you're not looking forward to the game.

Derek: Some people have a naturally serious face. Me, for instance.

Ed: In that case it might be a good idea to *work* at smiling now and then. I mean, why look unpleasant when you can look pleasant? Just put yourself in their shoes. What do the players want of the referee?

Derek: They want him to be crisp and clear and decisive. Also positive and constructive. They don't want a nit-picking whistle-blower. They want someone who'll help them make a game of it.

Ed: Someone they're confident in, and comfortable with.

Derek: That'll do.

Ed: If they sniff the slightest hint that he's nervous, or over-awed by the occasion, they'll be inclined to take advantage of that fact. If he comes across as domineering or authoritarian, then goodbye to any sense of friendly co-operation. If he's ingratiating and cracks jokes all the time, they'll suspect he might do anything to be popular, and that's a weakness just waiting to be exploited.

These are all judgements that can be made in a minute. And they can unmake the referee just as fast.

Ed: Be decisive. If you stop thinking – even for a few seconds – the players will start telling you what to do. Nobody expects the referee to be perfect, but if he makes his decisions crisply and quickly, the teams will respect and obey him. It's not enough to be right. You have to be right in the right manner.

Derek: So what's the answer? How does he win the game before the game?

Ed: Be relaxed, be natural, be in control, and enjoy yourself. Once they realise that you're there to make the match enjoyable if you can, then they will feel much more confident about doing the same. Whereas, if you seem edgy and suspicious and up-tight, they'll start wondering what's going to go wrong.

Derek: Insecurity is infectious.

Ed: It can be. What it comes down to is this: if the players aren't *for* you, they're *against* you. One of the greatest weapons in the referee's armoury is to be calm and quietly confident before the game. That's very reassuring to the players, because chances are they've had referees who virtually kicked down the dressing-room door, stopped the team talk and demanded to inspect the studs *right now*. And they did it in a grim sort of way, as if they were looking for trouble.

Derek: People who look for trouble invariably find it.

Ed: Of course they do.

Derek: So what's your approach?

Ed: Well, first I knock on the door and ask if I can come in. I ask the captain: 'When is it convenient for me to check the studs? When would you like to toss up?' And at the agreed time I'll also say whatever I have to say. Referees who barge in and give orders may think they're demonstrating their authority. What they're really doing is eroding the confidence of the players.

Derek: I remember referees like that from my playing days. They went onto the field looking like Caesar coming out to conquer Gaul. And they shouted like sergeant-majors.

Ed: We've got to move away from all that.

Derek: Now, I know that you always talk to all the front-row players before the match, instructing them how the scrum is to engage, but would you ever get the captains together and say, 'Listen, I expect you to lead your teams today and . . .'

Ed: Oh, I do that at every game! Whatever level I referee at, I always tell the captains, 'You're in control of your players. The way they behave is *your* responsibility, not mine. Now, if *you* can't deal with the way they behave, that means *I've* got to step in. And *I'm* not going to be very happy with *you*, and *you* could possibly not be very happy with *me* after I've dealt with it. So just you be aware of your responsibilities, because I'm totally aware of mine.'

Derek: Tone of voice matters when you say stuff like that.

Ed: Yes. It's not a lecture, it's a message. Firm but friendly. You want the players to feel comfortable – and at the same time to know that *you* are in control of this game. It may sound like a lot of little details, and that's what it is, but if you can't get all these little things right you'll never make it to the top. Never.

Derek: Still, it must help to be one of the best referees in the world, mustn't it? You haven't got to prove yourself.

Ed: So people keep telling me. My experience is, every referee has to prove himself every week. You're only as good as your last match. Besides, I wasn't always established. All international referees started from the same spot. I had to find my way through, like everyone else. Referees are all different. I had to find out what works for me.

'WE HAVEN'T GOT YOU, HAVE WE?'

Derek: Okay, here's the kind of thing a young referee comes across as he finds his way. He's been given a local game, he goes into the dressing-room to check studs, he knows half the team, and he knows that *they* know he did a rotten game the week before. He made a hash of it. 'Hullo!' they say. 'We haven't got you, have we? Bloody hell . . . That means a million penalty kicks this week, then . . . Trying to get in the Guinness Book of Records, are you?' And so on. Now, no matter how he behaves, they've got nil confidence in him. So what does he do?

Ed: He shakes it off.

Derek: You mean he keeps his mouth shut and goes away?

Ed: No. Look: refereeing's no different to playing – you have good games and bad games, and you must be honest about that.

Honest with yourself and with others. You don't leave it a week to say to people, 'Yes, I had a poor game last Saturday.' You put your hands up and admit it, and try to find out where you went wrong. Self-analysis can be painful, but it's essential if you're going to improve. It's too easy to blame the coach or the players or the weather. A good referee has got to be big enough to accept the fact that he's refereed a poor game, because only then can he identify his mistakes and start work on his faults that *caused* those mistakes.

So he mustn't hide from failure. He's got to face it, admit it, discuss it, understand it, and maybe a week later he'll be better equipped to referee again.

Derek: The hard fact remains: they all think he's crap.

Ed: Sure. So now he's got to work twice as hard to win their confidence. He can't just crumble. If you want to become a good referee, you've got to look the part: calm, competent, confident. You've got to go through the whole pre-match routine and look cheerful, and maybe they'll start to have a bit of confidence in you. You've *got* to get them on your side. For example, I never go out before the teams. Never. I always stand aside and say 'Good luck' to them as they run out. Then I follow. Now, that's not a ploy that I deliberately thought up. It just seemed the natural thing to do. But it does no harm.

THE GAME 'DURING'

Derek: Fine. We've got both teams on the pitch, so the game before the game is over. Let's assume they all have total faith, confidence and trust in you. From now on it's a piece of cake. Right?

Ed: Funnily enough, there are games like that – but not many. The reality is that you've got to keep on earning that confidence. And let's face it, nobody does a perfect game. We all get something wrong.

Derek: You wouldn't say that to the players, though, would you?

Ed: Oh, I would, yes. In big games, even international games, I've blown the whistle and then straightaway said to players,

'I've made a mistake, guys – you know it, I know it. Let's all start again.' And 99% of the time, people respect the fact that you've owned up. What they cannot abide, and will not accept, is when you try to gloss over a mistake. That's when they lose a bit of respect for you.

Derek: Would you say it even if the mistake was in or near the in-goal?

Ed: Without a doubt. There's no hiding from it.

Derek: Bang goes the chance for a try, perhaps. They're not going to like that.

Ed: Even more reason for honesty. The bigger the mistake, the more important it is to say so. Otherwise they begin to stop trusting you, and that's fatal. Players don't expect you to be perfect but they do expect you to be fair, and that means honest. Mind you, they won't forgive a whole string of mistakes! They'd prefer you to get it right and not have to apologise. There's no substitute for competence.

Derek: Let's assume that you're very competent and totally honest. That's all anybody can ask, isn't it? What else is there?

Ed: Sense of humour? If something funny happens – and rugby can be a very funny game – I see nothing wrong with the referee smiling or chuckling or bursting out laughing. And it just reminds the players: this guy's human, too. We're all on the same wavelength. Another thing I always do – and it wasn't a conscious decision, I just did it because I felt it was right – is when a player does something really well, I say, 'Well done! I enjoyed that.' Sometimes they look at you and you can see them think: *Oh! This referee understands a little bit about rugby.* I've done it at international level; I've said, 'Well played – that was good!'

CONFIDENCE IS EVERYTHING

Derek: Even if it's a try, and the opposition can hear you?

Ed: Yes. It's not a big statement, it's just a spontaneous remark, one more thing you do to try and make the players feel comfortable in your presence. Obviously what you *don't* do is tell them when they did something bad.

Derek: No, but I've heard you say 'Bad luck' when a nice-looking move didn't quite come off. I'd be afraid they might think I wasn't impartial.

Ed: Not if you've got their trust. You do what you feel is right. In a really fraught, grim sort of game, I might not say it. Or I might say it just to get them to relax a little bit.

Derek: Does it work in reverse? Does a player ever say 'Well done' to you?

Ed: Sometimes. Sometimes people actually turn round and say, 'Good decision, ref.' If I think it's sarcasm I just smile, but often you can see by the look in his eyes that he's genuine. And that's nice, because it shows that he's got confidence. With confidence both ways – yours to them, and theirs to you -you can overcome any problem. A few years ago I was refereeing Ireland versus Australia. One of the Australian props, Dan Crowley, collided with his own player and got a nasty gash in the lip and had to go off. Phil Kearns, their hooker, was captain. He said to me, 'Can we bring on the blood bin?' He meant a temporary replacement; in those days they allowed bleeding-player replacements in the Southern Hemisphere but I had to tell him we didn't, in the North. 'Ah, no!' he said. 'What do we do?' He wanted Crowley back on, once he'd been stitched up. I said, 'Look: move up your flanker, David Wilson.' Wilson was no prop, and Kearns said he wasn't going to be happy in the front row. I said: 'Just leave this with me, I'll deal with it.' Nick Popplewell was the Irish prop who would be facing Wilson. I told him what was happening. 'If you put any pressure on him, Nick, we might have to abandon the game.' Nick said, 'No problem, Ed, no problem!' So for three or four scrums Wilson just leaned against Nick, and Nick – being a practical man – didn't try to bend him. Then Crowley came on, stitched up, and we all got on with the real scrums for the rest of the game.

Derek: Were the scores close at the time?

Ed: No. But the game wasn't lopsided, either. Everybody used commonsense, and I was able to manage the situation because I was confident that I could, and Phil Kearns had confidence in me, and David Wilson – although he looked a bit cockled at me when I suggested he played prop – he had confidence in Kearns. And I think that if Popplewell hadn't felt comfortable with me as referee, he wouldn't have agreed.

Derek: Or maybe he would have agreed and then forgotten.

Ed: Exactly. After the match, at the dinner, the Australians thanked me. It was a classic case of all-round confidence getting us out of a difficult little situation.

Derek: We're now two-thirds of the way through your 3-Game Scenario. What's left to do?

THE GAME 'AFTER'

Ed: The game after the game is another crucial stage. This is when you must stay and make yourself available to the coaches and the players. In my opinion, they are my judges. They are my custodians. I've got to listen to them, answer their questions, take their suggestions on board. Obviously I don't accept every word they say – a team that's just lost isn't likely to have the same view as a team that's just won – but I always listen. Sometimes in the bar a player will say, 'Well, I didn't think you handled such-and-such today . . .' And I'll say, 'Look: you know and I know that I didn't have a very good game today.' They respect you for that. What they don't respect is referees who try to dodge admitting they got something wrong.

Derek: I can remember going into the bar and one team was too angry to speak to me.

Ed: It happens. A referee's got to be prepared to stay and face the music, even if it's silent! If I do a game and disallow a try, the coach might say afterwards, 'Look at the video, when you have a chance.' And I'll say, 'If the video proves me wrong, I'll phone you.' More than once I've phoned him and said, 'I watched the video. You're right, I made a mistake. This is just to say to you: I was in the wrong, and I apologise.' By now it's probably Tuesday or Wednesday and he's come down to earth a bit, and he'll say, 'Okay, I accept that, but you do realise that we've lost two points.' Or whatever.

Derek: Is this still part of the game after the game?

Ed: Yes. There are decisions to be made, long after you've blown the final whistle. People judge you on that behaviour.

Derek: Lose your temper with some dipstick in the bar, and you could blow everything in ten seconds.

Ed: Nobody said refereeing was easy. And the last impression is often the one that sticks longest.

In-Goal

Ed: I never have nightmares. In fact, once a game is over, I don't worry about it. But if I *did* have nightmares, they would be in the in-goal area.

Derek: Me too. It's the most important part of the field, because that's where tries are scored or saved. All the rest is just build-up.

Ed: The reality is that no referee ever does a perfect game, and if you make a slight mistake in midfield, it doesn't always matter, but if you make *any* kind of mistake in an in-goal, they won't forgive you in a hurry.

Derek: Especially if your mistake is being out of position.

Ed: They hate that, and quite rightly. They've done all the work, and if you don't see the try scored because you're in the wrong place – worst of all, if you're not in the in-goal at all – they find it very difficult to accept that. In-goal is an absolutely vital area. The referee must be totally concentrated. It should be every referee's aim and dream to be perfectly positioned, so that when the try-scorer looks up, he sees the referee looking down and signalling the try.

Derek: It's very satisfying when you anticipate where the attack is going and you get there first. Especially if the guy who scored is the fastest man on the field.

Ed: Exactly. And yet there *are* occasions when you can be perfectly positioned, but you still can't see the ball or the player grounding the ball. It's inevitable. Attackers and defenders are piling into each other, there may be a dozen bodies flying around in a very confined space, and it's all happening at very high speed. Sometimes the referee's view is bound to be obscured. You do your best but you can't see everything. Nobody can. Tries are scored but not given. It's not the referee's fault and he mustn't blame himself for it, because it's in the nature of the game.

Derek: That's not all, is it? There might be a ruck or a maul near the goal line, and the referee moves into the in-goal just in time to see an attacker come hurtling around the blind side and score. But what the referee *didn't* see was a colossal knock-on by that same attacker. He was rightly positioned for the try and wrongly positioned for the knock-on.

Ed: It happens.

Derek: So what's your advice? What should he have done?

Ed: Well, he's got to follow his own judgement.

Derek: That's a fat lot of good if he's a new referee. He hasn't *got* any judgement. He's never been in this situation before.

Ed: And that's how he'll learn. That's how you develop your judgement: you do it, and maybe get it slightly wrong, and you know better next time. Refereeing is something that can't be taught; it must be learned. Coaching helps, of course, but the referee has to go out and learn. On-the-job training is the only way.

Derek: All right. But what about this poor devil who's just missed a colossal knock-on? The defending team are very cheesed-off.

Ed: He didn't see the knock-on, so he can't blow for it. He did see the try, he's awarded it, so now he's got to get on with the game. Was his positioning right or wrong? I'd have to be there to answer that one. But there's another scenario, isn't there? Suppose he doesn't move into the in-goal, there *isn't* a knock-on, and now he can't see the try scored on the blind side. If that happened, I suggest that *both* teams would lose a lot of confidence in that referee. And it's all about confidence. It's not about perfection. It's about confidence.

Derek: Okay. Our referee is confident that the try was scored, but he's new to the whistle, he doesn't want to do anything stupid. In the summer he's a cricket umpire, and he's accustomed to just *thinking* for three or four seconds before he gives an LBW decision. So now he takes a good long look at this try, thinks hard, and then blows his whistle.

Ed: That's no good.

Derek: He's a thinker.

Ed: He's got to think faster. You must be *decisive* when you award a try or a touch-down. It's amazing the effect it has on people when you're decisive! They are far less prone to argue. Whereas if you wait . . . and wait . . . and wait . . . and then suddenly say, 'Try' – then everybody is aware that you're not sure. And the defending side feels hard done-by.

Derek: Even a two-second pause is a long time. *Five* seconds can be an eternity.

Ed: Exactly. Referees have to make very difficult decisions very quickly. Players want you to reach your decision fast and carry it out with an air of confidence. Be decisive and they'll accept your decision. Some of those decisions will be wrong, no matter what level you referee at. We've all been proved to have given tries when they probably weren't scored, and we've disallowed tries that maybe were perfectly good. The wheel of fortune goes around and in the end the luck probably balances out. Meanwhile, be decisive. It's a sign that you're in control. Players want that. Start looking indecisive and there's a danger they might start taking a few decisions for themselves.

Derek: Let's get back to in-goal play. What are your priorities? What matters most?

Ed: Well, there's quite a bit of law governing the in-goal, and it's obviously essential to know it all inside-out. Given that, I have a simple approach. If I'm sure he's scored, I give the try. If I'm sure he hasn't scored, I don't give a try. If I'm not sure what happened, then I give a 5-metre scrum. Now I know that sounds very simplistic, almost not worth saying because it's so obvious. But I think the in-goal is so important that the simpler the better, because it allows the referee to focus sharply on what is absolutely crucial.

You must do what you think is honest and right. If there's *any* doubt in my mind, I'll scrummage five. If I'm not sure that the ball was grounded – scrummage five. If I'm not sure which player actually grounded the ball first – scrummage five. And let the attacking side have the put-in. Put like that, it may sound easy. Sometimes it's not.

Derek: You mean the pressure on the referee from the players . . .

Ed: It can be immense. It's not that they are out to bamboozle him or con him – although one or two might – it's simply that they get swept along by the speed and the excitement of it all, the sheer drama, and so you've got fifteen guys who desperately *want* you to give a try, and another fifteen guys who desperately want the opposite. There is a lot of tension in the air.

Derek: Not to mention fifty thousand screaming spectators.

Ed: It calls for mental strength by the referee to resist all that pressure, to ignore it and concentrate on making the honest, correct decision. It's not easy.

Derek: We all like to be liked.

Ed: Too true. But we're not there to be liked. The in-goal can be a very lonely place, especially for a young referee who wants to make a success of the game. Later on, of course, he might have the benefit of touch judges.

Derek: You're talking about qualified touch judges, aren't you? Team-of-Three stuff?

Ed: They can be a tremendous help when play gets near or inside the in-goal.

Derek: What do you ask them to do?

Ed: When a try might – or might not – have been scored, I look directly at the nearest touch judge. He knows what I want is a decisive indication: *Yes,* or *No,* or *Not Sure.* I don't mind which I get, as long as it's fast and clear. If I'm not sure, and the touch judge is not sure, then we'll scrummage five. So it's very simple. But no delay. A quick glance from me, a signal from him, and bingo! Decision. Usually, of course, I don't need his confirmation because most tries are clear-cut. All the same, what I *don't* want him to do is run around behind the posts. Not immediately. A few years ago it was standard practice for them to sprint into the

Ed: A referee must be fit, and that includes being mentally strong. When a try is (or isn't) scored, he's likely to be on the receiving end of colossal pressure. Fifteen guys desperately want him to say one thing. Fifteen guys desperately want the opposite. He must ignore them all, do what's right and stick to it. Half of them will hate him. That's okay. He's not out there to make friends.

in-goal. Why? It's not necessary. I've seen a touch judge almost reach the posts before he realised the referee hadn't awarded a try at all! So I tell my touch judges to stand their ground for a moment, until they're sure that I have signalled a try. Otherwise they might look foolish.

Derek: And they might cast doubt on the referee's decision.

Ed: That, too.

Derek: I don't think spectators realise what a tough job touch-judging can be. When a winger's going flat-out for the corner, the touch judge has to keep pace with him *and* watch the winger's feet *and* watch the ball *and* watch the corner flag.

Ed: Those are the most difficult decisions for a touch judge to make. Did the player put a foot into touch? If he did, was it before or after he grounded the ball? Did he touch the corner flag or touch-in-goal before he grounded the ball? Did he really ground the ball, or did he lose it?

Derek: And it all happens in a flash. The winger's diving, a tackler's flying in from the side . . .

Ed: It's more than the referee can handle. Sean Fitzpatrick was asked if he felt the game needed two referees now. 'No,' he said. 'Referees do a difficult job, and on the whole I think they do it very well.' Nice to hear something positive! But at senior level we're totally reliant on good touch judges. From time to time, if the touch judge hadn't been in a position to see the try, I wouldn't have been able to give it.

Derek: Meanwhile, of course, down in the depths of the game, the referee's lucky if he's got any touch judges at all. Often he has none. Any advice?

IT'S NOT YOUR PROBLEM

Ed: Go back to the captains. It's their duty to provide touch judges. If literally nobody is available, tell the captains that you expect to get their players' co-operation when the ball goes into touch. If that doesn't work, tell the captains to choose one player each and make him touch judge. Find a way to manage the situation. But don't let the problem weigh you down. It's not *your* problem. It's *their* problem. If mistakes are made because there are no touch judges, that's their responsibility, not yours.

Derek: A lot of young referees – and some old ones – pick up tricks of the trade from watching rugby on television. For instance, they see top referees in the in-goal getting very low. Sometimes they kneel. Sometimes they're on their hands and knees!

Ed: Alan Hosie was a great exponent of kneeling and looking for the ball, usually when it was arriving at a very low altitude! It you feel it helps, do it. It comes down to what you feel *natural* with. Obviously it doesn't come natural to me, because I've never done it. So I suppose the problem has never arisen. Where I *have* had a problem is with pitch markings near the goal line. Anyone who has refereed in Paris knows that the soccer markings are quite visible.

Derek: The grass never grows long enough to cover them.

Ed: And the speed of the game is such that it's very easy to slip up and mistake a soccer line for a goal line. It can also happen without soccer markings. When I refereed in Cumbria not long ago, a guy got the ball and dived over the 5-metre line.

Derek: Thought he'd scored?

Ed: He cheered! And I could see the opposition relax, so I think they felt he'd scored, as well. Because it was a genuine mistake, I said: 'We'll scrummage – attacking side's ball.'

Derek: Who needs the 5-metre line, anyway? Only the referee. It's there to help him with 5-metre scrums and penalty kicks, that's all. It doesn't have to be white. The law simply says it must be 'suitably marked out'. So it could be red or blue. Then the players would be less likely to mistake it for the goal line.

Ed: That's not a bad idea.

Derek: I have one, every ten or twelve years.

Ed: I refereed on a pitch where the groundsman hadn't made the breaks in the 5-metre line nearly long enough. It looked almost continuous, with just a few gaps. Not surprisingly a player went over the 5-metre, thinking it was the goal line. I couldn't give the try, and his team lost. They were not well pleased.

Derek: That sort of thing is always likely to happen in junior clubs. I've come across unequal in-goals – one twice as deep as the other – and dead-ball lines that faded and disappeared into nothing. Come to that, I've taken games where the goal lines wandered drunkenly across the pitch.

Ed: Certainly, part of the referee's pre-match procedure should be to walk around and look at the pitch. If you find the kind of problem you described, and it can't be put right, tell the captains before the game. Even at senior level, I always check. I was getting ready to referee Harlequins versus Orrell in London, and I saw the goal line at one end was very faint. Heavy overnight rain washed it out. The groundsman remarked it, quickly and efficiently, and just as well he did, because two tries were scored in that very area.

Derek: And since a try can be scored *on* the goal line . . .

Ed: On the line! So, pre-match, a referee should always walk around the ground. Check how soft or hard it is, the type of grass, look for any potholes, ask the groundsmen to fill them in with some sand. It might not be a player's ankle that breaks – it could be yours. Which is quite important. And especially, check out the in-goals. They can vary enormously. In the Army Stadium at Aldershot they're very small, only about 5 metres deep. At other grounds they're the full 22 metres deep. That's room for an awful lot of play. If a kick at goal fails, the ball still has 22 metres to roll.

Derek: Which is a considerable distance.

Ed: And if you're not aware of it, you could really catch a cold.

Derek: Everything you've said applies at junior clubs, and more. I always have a good look around. It's amazing what people leave lying on the pitch: beer cans, bottles, lengths of wood, small change, portable phones . . . The biggest thing I ever found was a steel wheelbrace.

Ed: Not what your average three-quarter wants to land on when he's tackled!

Derek: Could be painful! And since the in-goals are always likely to see violent action, I always take a very close look there.

A Bad Day at the Office

Ed: I remember taking the Pilkington Cup Final in 1994, Bath versus Leicester. That was a poor game. After twenty minutes I knew I wasn't refereeing well – and I was working very hard to get better! But it was just one of those occasions when it was going to be a bad day at the office. There are days like that. Unfortunately, there were 68,000 people in the ground and millions watching on TV. I suppose the answer is to choose your bad days a bit better.

Derek: But you can't, can you? You may wake up that morning feeling fine, you're really looking forward to the game – and from the kick-off it just doesn't come good.

Ed: Nobody can say why. In every walk of life, people have good days and bad. Rob Andrew was a fine player, and I've refereed games where Rob missed kicks in front of the posts. It was a bad day at the office for him, and referees are no different from players: you're not going to do well every week, even when you're at the top. Referees have got to accept that fact, and learn to live with it. Bath-Leicester was a poor game and I take my share of responsibility for it. I did at the time.

Derek: Yes, but that was *after* the match. What did you do during it, to try to jack up your performance?

Ed: The first thing I had to do – and it's not as easy as it sounds – was actually *recognise* that things weren't going well.

Derek: Being a bit sluggish gets in the way of realising how sluggish you are?

Ed: Something like that. And the less experience you have, the harder it is to identify that the problem is *you*, not them.

Derek: So what are the clues to look for?

Ed: Players are good judges. They go onto the field expecting you to do your job. But they won't be impressed by your reputation, and if after five minutes they think, *Hullo, he's not refereeing that part of the game today,* they'll be in like a shot.

Derek: They can sniff it out as fast as that?

Ed: Oh, there's a lot of clever people around! If you won't control the game, they won't hesitate to do it for you. And then you'll have a problem, because whatever happens, *you* must always be controlling *them.* And if the captain's constantly coming up to you and saying things like: 'Have a look at their back row at the ruck – they're offside all the time', and you think: *This guy doesn't normally try to pressurise me* – that's when you might suspect you're having a bad day at the office.

Derek: And what can you do about it?

Ed: Go back to basics.

Derek: Which means . . .

Ed: Start again. The first thing I would say to myself would be: *Start all over again. Let's pretend the game starts now.* And I'd say: *You've not refereed the scrum – start refereeing it now. Whatever you let happen in the first ten minutes – forget that! Go back to your basics.*

Derek: You're saying all this to yourself. What are you telling the players?

Ed: At the next scrum, I'd say 'Right! Wait there until I'm ready. Crouch. Blue hooker – look up. Red loosehead, keep your shoulders up.' I'd start to get a little bit finicky, I'd referee a lot firmer, I'd remind them who's in control here. I'd find ways of slowing things down a bit. When the line-out formed, I'd tell the hooker not to throw in. I'd tell them I wanted a wider gap. I'd spend more time at the front, where they could see me. Slowing it down a bit lets me work harder, and that gets my thought-processes ticking over faster, until I've found my confidence again.

Derek: Would all this back-to-basics stuff affect the way you play advantage?

Ed: It might. A lot depends on the situation. If a game has become very loose and untidy and I feel I'm losing control of it, I'll tighten up on advantage. Later, I can let play stretch again.

A PIECE OF ELASTIC

Derek: This idea of allowing the game to stretch, or not: it's right at the heart of your understanding of rugby, isn't it?

Ed: You referee on a piece of elastic, and not on a piece of string. That's important, I think. But it's equally important to realise that the referee does not dictate how the game is played. The *players* dictate.

Derek: The referee can never be a sort of puppet-master.

Ed: Never. It should never enter his mind. Rugby is a players' game, they dictate how it's played, and as a result they dictate my decision-making process. If both teams want a very tight, fraught game played at close quarters, then I'll have to work hard to keep a tight rein on them.

Derek: More string than elastic.

Ed: Not much elastic, certainly. Whereas, if they all want to get the ball into play quickly and run it around the field, that's when the elastic stretches. And it can stretch quite a lot, provided you're impartial and consistent. It's no good letting the elastic stretch for one team but not the other.

Derek: Bang goes their confidence in you.

Ed: Exactly.

Derek: Now, you've described one version of a bad day at the office. I can describe a completely different one, where the referee did a very competent job but maybe one team hated him, or the crowd hated him, or both. Now that's not much fun.

Ed: I distinguish between the teams and the crowd. The spectators have paid their money and if they want to bawl at me all afternoon, that is their prerogative. Inevitably, they'll some-times be not very happy with me. I've been spat at, I've been escorted off the pitch by the police when I've refereed abroad, and that's sad; but the reality is that people in different countries have different cultures, and what we might consider unacceptable is quite normal behaviour to them.

Derek: Touch judges usually zero-in on the referee at the end.

Ed: Yes, and the security organisation at internationals is such that you're usually safe from spectators. The ideal situation is to blow the final whistle by the players' entrance!

Derek: As you're walking off, several very angry players want to challenge your decisions. They have many questions they want answered. They believe you lost them the match.

Ed: My philosophy's quite simple. No matter how good or bad a game you had, you always face the music. You always answer to the players. But not on the pitch! Later.

Derek: Well, these guys won't accept that. They're not going to be fobbed off.

Ed: Tough luck. They're on an emotional high. Whatever I say, it won't satisfy them, and I may live to regret saying it. So I'm not going to discuss anything with anybody until I've showered and dressed and made my way to the players' bar.

Derek: One player is so disgusted that he calls you a cheat, with several obscenities before and after.

Ed: That counts as misconduct under the Foul Play Law, even though the final whistle's gone, so he's in big trouble.

NEVER TRY TO EVEN THINGS UP

Derek: Okay. Now *you* can cope with all this pressure, because you've been there, seen it, done it all before. What about the young and up-and-coming referee? All his games are satisfactory – hard but enjoyable – until one day he finds himself slightly out of his depth. Halfway through the game, he starts to worry: maybe his mistakes have lost this match for one team. It's not too late to make good . . .

Ed: That's fatal. Absolutely fatal. He must never think like that. Never. At the most junior level – at every level – you've got to make the decision you think is correct. Nobody, but nobody, should ever be able to accuse the referee of cheating. Perhaps they can say he didn't know his law, or he wasn't fit, or his positioning was bad, but never that he was cheating. If a referee ever gets into the habit of making decisions based on what he *thinks* happened, or what he thinks *ought* to happen, then he's on a knife-edge and he'll be found out. Simple as that. Players won't respect you for trying to even things up. They'll only respect you if they think you're absolutely straight.

Derek: Okay. No argument about that. But let's look at a similar scenario. No crowd problems here; just a handful of spectators. What we've got is a very junior referee taking a 3rd XV match between two very contrasting teams. One has a lot of youngsters and they're not very big. The other has a load of old sweats who are smacking their lips at the prospect of hammering these kids.

Ed: How does the referee know that?

Derek: He changed in the same room as the old sweats. The game starts, within ten minutes the kids have scored two good tries and —

Ed: And the old sweats don't like it.

Derek: They hate it. They hate the opposition, they hate the referee, and from then on they give him a lot of flak. And when he concentrates his attention on them, they complain that he's not impartial. In a sense, he *isn't* impartial – he's watching one team very carefully, far more carefully than the other.

Ed: But their behaviour is absolutely deliberate. I mean, they're making a deliberate attempt to influence that referee's decision-making. If all the problems are coming from one team, of course he must pay them more attention. As referees, we all go through the learning curve of coping with people who keep trying to influence us.

Derek: It's almost intimidation. If they protest loudly enough when they're penalised, maybe a slightly insecure referee will hesitate next time.

Ed: Exactly. They'll shout for everything. I hate people who constantly appeal, it reminds me too much of soccer. Very often I say, 'If you appeal again, I'll ignore what happened.' And of course sometimes they'll appeal when they know you didn't see it – and if you blow up and give it, *they know they've got you*. And they'll milk you dry. This problem will never go away. With the change in the game at senior level, referees are going to be under more and more pressure. While I'm a great believer in dialogue, that doesn't mean a player can tell me when and why to blow the whistle. He'll try. Referees have got to be mentally strong; very strong.

Derek: So what's your advice to the young referee who took that 3rd XV game?

Ed: Well, it's a classic example of the way pressure makes some people's personalities change. The nice, friendly guys in the dressing-room suddenly grow horns. Their behavioural habits change for the worse. There's only one answer to that. You've got to jump on them at a very early stage. Get a solid grip. If you don't – if after twenty minutes they're still up to no good – and *then* you try to stop it . . . Well, you've got a massive problem on your hands.

Derek: All right: suppose the referee jumps on them, gets an early grip on the game. It's not a happy outlook, is it? One team hates him, because they're losing the match and he's watching them like a hawk. The game's hardly begun and he's got fifteen blokes not looking forward to the rest of the afternoon.

Ed: Some referees make the mistake: they actually want to be *liked*. Now, there's a big difference between being *liked* and being *respected*. I tell referees: 'Your sole job out there is to be respected by thirty players.' And if fifteen people don't like you, and fifteen do, that's absolutely immaterial, as long as all thirty respect what you're doing. If anybody starts refereeing in order to become Mr Popular Nice Guy, he really ought to be thinking about doing something else.

Derek: Okay. The good news is that our hypothetical young referee gets an early grip, makes them respect him, and just dogs it out to the end. Now he's got to walk a quarter of a mile to the clubhouse. And immediately he's surrounded by spectators, all

Ed: Sometimes it's a long walk from the pitch to the clubhouse after the final whistle, with spectators all around you, shouting and cursing. There's only one thing to do. Ignore them. Say nothing. Anything you say will only make matters worse. Don't even look at them. Keep walking. You've done your job. They'll soon get fed up and quit. Think of the hot shower waiting for you. You deserve it.

shouting, telling him what he did wrong, telling him he's the worst bloody ref they've ever bloody seen and he ought to throw his bloody whistle in the bloody river.

Ed: And that's just the women!

Derek: Correct! He sets off, and they follow. The insults get worse.

Ed: My experience is, the best thing to say to angry spectators is exactly nothing. In fact, nothing is the *only* thing to say. Just look straight ahead and don't stop. Whatever you say to an angry spectator will only make him angrier. It can be tempting to put him straight, or to put him down, but if you try, you'll only add fuel to the fire. He's not listening. Never talk to people who aren't listening. Keep your mouth shut and head for the showers. You've done your job. Arguing with angry spectators is not your job.

Derek: That walk from the pitch to the clubhouse can be a real test of self-control for a referee.

Ed: Yes, it can. What he should be saying to himself is: *Just because this guy behaves like an idiot is no reason for me to behave like an idiot as well.* If someone's talking rubbish, why flatter him by answering? Say nothing. Keep walking. Pretend he doesn't exist, and very soon he *won't* exist.

Line-Out

Derek: One of the bits of useless information that every spectator seems to know is that a maximum of 94 offences can be committed at any one line-out. Or it might be 89, or 103. The list gets longer as the beer goes down.

Ed: The line-out law is certainly the longest in the book, by far.

Derek: That's what baffles a lot of people. If it's such a legal jungle, how can you possibly referee it?

Ed: I've got two priorities: space and protection. Before the ball is thrown, there must be a space one metre wide between the two lines of players. I'm looking for them to *keep* that space as long as possible. Then, once the ball is thrown in, I want to give as much protection as possible to the players who want to *move into* that space to try to jump for the ball. Provided you can keep space – and that's all the jumper wants; he wants an opportunity to move into space with a little help from his team but no obstruction from the opposition – provided you can do *that*, then you've really achieved almost everything you can achieve.

Derek: I suppose it goes without saying that you want the ball thrown in straight.

Ed: Yes. I want the throw-in to be a fair contest for the ball.

Derek: And what about the other 92 or 85 offences, or whatever the true number is?

Ed: If they make no difference to the game, I pay them no attention. So many things happen at a line-out, you could carry on blowing all day long, if you wanted. The top coaches and players and referees in England met in 1995 and put together the Trent Agreement. It's common sense and it's been largely accepted all around the world. What we've said about the line-out is that if a lesser offence takes place, say at the front – for instance, opposing players grapple with each other, but no foul play occurs – and the ball is thrown to the back and won cleanly, then let's carry on. If a team can get the ball away from the line-out after a fair contest, then let's not worry about minor infringements. Let's allow the line-out to do its job, which is to get the ball back into play as quickly and fairly as possible. If there's space for the jumper to move into, and if he can do that without being interfered with by the opposition, then we've enabled him to compete for the ball.

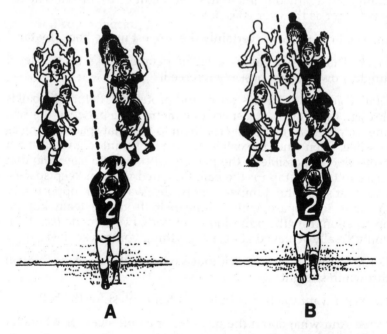

A   **B**

Ed: At the line-out I want two things above all: good space for the jumpers to jump into, and protection for them when they jump. Space means keeping a clear gap one metre wide between the two lines, as shown on the left. If an opponent moves into this gap, as shown on the right, the jumper has no space to jump into. So I watch that space very carefully. Without it, the line-out can't begin to work properly.

Derek: It seems to me that, as a referee, you're pre-selecting which part of the line-out to concentrate on, before the ball's been thrown in. You're saying to yourself: Forget *that* lot, let's look at *this* lot.

Ed: The reality is that you can't watch everyone. If Martin Bayfield's playing for Northampton, on their throw-in I would be concentrating on him. He's six foot ten; there's not too many people making a clean jump against Martin Bayfield who would win the ball. So maybe – just maybe – the only way his opponents can win the ball is to knock him slightly, or pull his arm as he's going up. There are all sorts of things they can do to spoil his jump.

Derek: Isn't it possible that his jump might be spoiled quite legally? When both he and an opponent jump for a ball, they're trying to occupy the same space. Isn't it inevitable they will bump each other?

Ed: Not inevitable, but it often happens. Then what I'm looking for is *intent*. Did that player go up for the ball, or did he go up intending to knock his opponent?

Derek: Maybe he did both. There are some cunning buggers out there.

KEEP THE GAP

Ed: Well, that's why you've got to concentrate. And if a Martin Bayfield keeps coming down empty-handed time after time, you've got to ask yourself, why? Maybe he's not being given the space to jump into. This is one of the big problems of the line-out. The opposition will try to *close down* the jumper's space. If the ball's thrown in straight, it travels along the line-of-touch, this imaginary line between the two sets of forwards. Well, maybe the opposition will move a body into a hole on that line, or maybe they'll simply step across the line as the ball's thrown, closing the gap, leaving the jumper no room to jump. You usually find that when you've got a problem at the line-out, it's because the gap has been closed. New Zealand do it very well. On the opposition ball, all seven men close the gap. Now the opposition have got no space to jump in. They end up jumping where the ball is *not*. Making sure a team doesn't close down the space is the hardest part of the line-out, I think. Because all the jumper wants is an opportunity to move into that space.

Derek: All right. So establishing the metre gap is a top priority. How do you set about it?

Ed: If you can get the first two guys in the line on your side and assisting you, you probably haven't got a problem.

Derek: These are the front markers from each team? Usually props?

Ed: Yes. Just before the '95 World Cup, when the IRB had ruled that the stepaway was illegal – they weren't going to allow a team to take a step away from the line-out and then all step back as the ball was thrown, it was very messy – I had a long discussion with Jimmy Fleming. He said that, as referees, we'd become very lazy. We were allowing players to create space for us – and of course doing it to suit themselves – instead of us refereeing the line-out the way *we* wanted it. I disagreed with him then. I don't now. I think Jim's right. I think our prime task is to create space for the jumpers to move into, unobstructed. So – to get back to the front markers – the first thing I always do is have a quiet word with these two props and say: 'You're the assistant referees today. You referee the line-out for me. You insist that there's a proper gap, and you insist that your guys are straight on you. Do that, please, and everything will be wonderful.'

Derek: You say this before the match?

Ed: No. At the first line-out. It's usually the same two props all through the game. If I can get them on my side, that's a very good start.

Derek: It still leaves a hell of a lot for the referee to look for, doesn't it? Just to pick out a few things: you've got to watch the ball in case somebody knocks-on, and while you're looking high, you've got to watch down below for opponents grabbing the jumper's legs, and then he might miss the ball, it might go to the tail, so you've got to be prepared for that too. You're watching fourteen men, spread over ten yards. Where do you stand? How do you position yourself?

Ed: At the first line-out I tell the front markers (usually props) to stand one metre apart and make sure their players line up on them. If they can keep good space, that's one less job for me to do. Usually I stand behind the player throwing in and slightly to one side of him. Now I'm looking down the tunnel, checking that the space remains open. I've got further to run, but that's worth it if the line-out can be made to work.

Ed: For most line-outs, and certainly for the first two or three, I normally stand behind the hooker throwing in.

Derek: When I took up refereeing, that's where I was told *not* to stand. Mind you, I was also told not to talk to the players . . .

Ed: Some assessors believe referees should stand at the front, at the middle, or at the back. I argue that where they stand is almost immaterial, provided they're comfortable and in control! Nowadays you'll see more and more referees operating at the front of the line-out than ever before. I'm much more comfortable there. I take up an unusual position – some assessors don't like it – in that I'm actually *behind* the player throwing in.

Derek: What's the advantage?

Ed: Several advantages. The main one is that I'm looking straight down the tunnel, everybody's looking towards me, and I've got this vision of exactly when and how the space is eroded. I'm sure in my mind of who's closing that space down. And I want to impress on the players that this is what I'm looking for. They can

Ed: Line out jumpers need protection from the dirty tricks which the opposition can use to try to spoil their efforts. Here's one. The White player grabs his opponent's inside arm. This not only prevents a two-handed catch; it also destroys the jumper's balance. Even if he gets a hand on the ball, he may be unable to control it. New referees often make the mistake of watching the ball – and so they miss the action going on beneath it.

see me, they can see what I want. If I can keep players on *their* side of the line-out, a lot of other things get tidied up.

Derek: This is preventative refereeing, by the sound of it. You're trying to *avoid* blowing your whistle.

Ed: Yes. It's all about priorities. When you take up refereeing, you just need to ask yourself some questions. At a line-out, what are we trying to achieve? We're trying to get the ball away, and as quickly as possible. The ball off the top is the best ball for *everybody* in the game: a clean catch, back to scrum-half, out to fly-half and we're off and running! How to achieve that? Well, somebody's got to jump for the ball, so he must be *allowed* to jump for it. And that's always been my priority: allowing that guy the opportunity to jump for the ball.

TROUBLE AT THE TAIL

Derek: Okay. That's your central priority. But there's more to the line-out than jumpers, isn't there? What about hanky-panky at the tail?

Ed: Oh, certainly. There may be overstepping by a flanker at the back or by a prop or hooker at the front. By crossing the line they show themselves to the opposition's scrum-half. Even if they step back again, he's not likely to make a break in *that* particular direction, so they've cut down his options.

Derek: By going a little bit offside.

Ed: Exactly. Or the flanker may step over the 15-metre line. Now he's got an advantage when he goes for their No. 10. Maybe it's only a metre, but . . .

Derek: That could be the difference between making and missing a tackle.

Ed: Easily. So, once I'm confident the line-out is going reasonably well and the jumpers are getting the opportunity to win the ball, then I'll move to my next priority and have a look at the back. Space is important there, too. Flankers – especially the No. 7's – get a better angle of run if they can close the gap. If you're always at the front, you're not going to see this. And similarly, if you *have* got a problem with the front-jumpers clattering into each other, it's no good being at the back. You need to be where you can see and identify what's going on. What's almost as important, they can actually see *you*! I like eye contact. You can give a wink or a nod, get your point across. I'm also very conscious of, not so much *listening* to players, as picking up the vibes from them. That's very important at a line-out, especially when the ball's been won and gone away. If nobody's moaning and whingeing and trying to smash his opposite number, you can feel the line-out's going reasonably well. If there's a sort of aftermath of bad temper, there's usually a reason.

Derek: You haven't said anything about the middle.

Ed: I'm not an advocate of standing near the middle of the line-out. I can't see what I want to see. Jim Fleming is so tall that he's comfortable wherever he stands. Because I'm not tall – only five foot ten – and because of the colossal *size* of these guys, it's much harder for me. There's another reason. Some very sharp gents are playing this game, with a very cute sense of humour. If the hooker sees you standing at the middle of the line, he just might throw the ball where his guys can clatter into you, just for fun.

Derek: A wise old bird once told me that if there was trouble brewing at the line-outs but I didn't know who was causing it, I should walk up the tunnel and look every player in the eye. 'Maybe they'll think you know more than you do,' he said.

Ed: I wouldn't do that. I certainly would never go in there on a whim. That's almost as dangerous as standing between the front rows of the scrum. If I had to go in, I'd tell the hooker not to throw the ball *and* I'd say to the touch judge, 'Please do not allow the hooker to throw the ball in. Lower your flag and wait until I'm ready.' Then I'd tell the players whatever I've got on my mind. You need to be very careful in those situations.

Derek: You do talk to players at the line-out, though. I've watched you. At virtually every line-out you're putting somebody straight about something.

Ed: Often it's nothing to do with the line-out. The great thing about the line-out is that it gives us the opportunity as referees to talk, to communicate, to manage. For instance, I might say: 'No. 6 – I saw you at that last scrum – you slip your binding again and I *will* penalise you.' The modern game has become so fast that I might not have *time* to say that at the next scrum.

Derek: Especially if you're asking for a quick feed.

Ed: Exactly. What with quick free kicks, quick penalties, quick throw-ins, quick drop-outs, there are very few pauses in the game, just brief moments the referee can use to slide in a bit of information that might save him having to blow up and give a penalty later. The formed line-out is the one occasion when you can even *make* some time. You say to the hooker, 'Can you give me a second, please.' Then you make your point to a player or maybe tell the captain he's got a problem he'd better sort out. Then you tell the hooker, 'Right – away you go.' It's only a matter of a few seconds but if we don't make the most of these brief opportunities, we're losing out as referees.

Derek: If the match is played on a park pitch and the ball's kicked into the tennis courts, the referee might have quite a long time to say his piece. Long enough to explain the offside law, even.

Ed: Long enough to try, anyway.

SHORT-CHANGED AGAIN

Derek: One of the irritating little things about the line-out is the throw-in that doesn't go five metres. When it happens in international matches, the referee blows up – so he's obviously seen it. But he never penalises. Just a scrum. The law couldn't be clearer: preventing the throw-in going five metres is a free kick offence. I penalise it, down in the grassroots, so why don't the big boys?

Ed: If they see it, they should penalise it. But unless I can clearly see that a front marker has gone forward and taken the ball within the five, I'll give him the benefit of the doubt. It's the good old honesty factor: if you're not in a position to see something, *don't give it*. Never penalise what you can't see. At senior level I'll be saying to my touch judge, 'If I'm missing things, tell me,' and he might say, 'That prop's taking the ball early, it's not in five.' It's another example of why I like to be at the front. I'm not going to see that offence from the back – and it's no coincidence that (apart from short line-outs) when I move to the back, the ball never goes there!

Derek: Makes you think, doesn't it?

Ed: Let's be honest: sides *know* where I am. Most teams will have a signal to say where the referee's standing.

Derek: Really? How do they signal?

Ed: Oh, it could be a name, it could be anything.

Derek: So if they shout 'Stoke-on-Trent', that's not necessarily the signal for the throw-in at all?

Ed: 'Stoke' could be where the ball's going, but 'Trent' could be where the referee's stood!

[LAUGHTER]

If they can entice you to the back and throw the ball four metres, they could win quick possession and be away! The reality is, this is what you're up against as a referee. If they get away with it, that's one up to them. Assessors often say in reports: *Don't be predictable at line-outs. Don't always stand in the same spot.* I totally agree. If I'm at the front, all of a sudden I'll skip down to the back. If I'm at the back on the attacking side, just before the ball's thrown I'll step over to the defending side. You must never be still at a line-out.

Derek: Agreed. Now, you've said you don't like a messy scrum, you want it tight and tidy. That's not true of the other set piece, is it? The line-out can be very messy – all that frantic changing of places, all those guys getting flung in the air. How d'you feel about that?

'EARLY SUPPORT'

Ed: If the line-out looks a bit peculiar now, just remember what it was like ten or fifteen years ago! It was a jungle. Players clattered into their opposite numbers, irrespective of where the ball was going.

Derek: Especially the props at the front.

Ed: They just went *crash*, straight into each other. And of course the jumpers had a very hard time finding space. Let's face it, there was a lot of skulduggery in all that confusion.

Derek: So the law was changed.

Ed: And one crucial difference is that now line-out players are not allowed to lay hands on their opponents except in a ruck or maul. Secondly, there must be a gap a metre wide when the ball is thrown. Those two facts give the jumpers space to operate without getting knocked about. Result: better, quicker possession.

Derek: So far, so good. Now we get to the airborne bit. Let's be clear about this: as long as the jumper is in the air, he can't be tackled, can he?

Ed: Correct. This is a health-and-safety thing. We can't have players six feet off the ground getting grabbed by the ankles. It's obviously dangerous.

Derek: So team-mates who helped him up must also help to let him down safely, as soon as the ball's won. No holding him up indefinitely. And this is their legal responsibility.

Ed: Safety again. Of course, the jumper doesn't always come down holding the ball – often he passes to his scrum-half while he's still up high. It's fast, clean possession, very effective. But even when he's passed it off the top, his opponents can't manhandle him as he comes down. His safety is paramount. Line-out jumpers reach phenomenal heights nowadays. Often the ball's 12 feet above the ground when it's caught.

Derek: Sure. And those jumpers couldn't possibly get up there without a lot of help. This is where the lawbook seems to be on another planet.

Ed: For instance.

Derek: Well, for a start it says a line-out player must not *pre-grip* any team-mate below the waist – 'pre-grip' meaning 'hold his shorts before he jumps'. Then it says a player must not *support* this team-mate *in any way* before he jumps. And even when he's jumped, the law says he must not *lift* a team-mate. It's a triple whammy, isn't it? No pre-grip, no lifting, and not much support! But that's not what I see happening, week in, week out. When the line-out forms, two strong men grip the guy's shorts, or the tape around his thighs, and as the ball's thrown they boost him up like an express elevator. And everyone's happy with that.

Ed: It's become a spectacular part of the game.

Derek: Somebody described the line-out law on lifting as 'ambiguous', which I think is a charitable way of saying that lifting may be illegal but it works, so let's turn a blind eye to the law.

Ed: There's no doubt that the interpretation has been very flexible! It's what coaches, players and administrators want, and they're satisfied with it. It's more constructive, more creative. There's far more clean ball coming away from the line-out, and from the refereeing point of view, what makes life much easier is the fact that now, with early support, we've got players from each side with their hands on *their own* players – not on the opposition. The point is, when we looked at the *practicalities* of actually refereeing that aspect of the game, we knew we *had* to find a way of improving the line-out. If we didn't do it, the lawmakers would. They'd either ban the line-out or turn it into something unrecognisable and it would be lost. So I think this was a practical approach.

Derek: At first there was a lot of worry about the safety angle, wasn't there? Fear that a big jumper might get tipped sideways and fall badly.

Ed: Or that a small jumper might get fired too high! But teams have acted sensibly. When they help a man up, they must help him down too.

Derek: Occasionally the whole line-out goes wrong and it looks like a cheap circus act.

Ed: You mean the jumpers go up but the ball isn't thrown? Shambles. Big men held up in the sky, waiting for nothing, is bad news. Usually the thrower's fault for delay. I'd penalise him.

Derek: Another line-out law that used to get people steamed-up was the 'inside arm' requirement. Not a problem any more?

Ed: Originally it said the jumper must use only his inside arm to catch the ball or knock it back. The thinking was that if he used his outside arm, the inside arm might be up to all kinds of foul play, like levering on an opponent. Trouble was, the 'inside arm only' law stopped the jumper using both hands to catch the ball, so it was changed to let him do that. If only one hand, it must be the inside arm. No problem.

Derek: I'll tell you an issue that can be contentious: numbers. Especially at the junior level. That's the one thing they can all do – count the players in the line-out!

Ed: And they're used to telling us, aren't they?

[LAUGHTER]

Derek: They don't get much change out of me. I just say: 'Advantage applies – now shut up!'

Ed: It rarely ever happens, at senior level. People sometimes get confused when the team with the throw-in calls a two-man line-out, and the opposition pulls out everyone except two locks and a No. 8. So someone shouts, 'Numbers, numbers!' What he's forgetting is the No. 8 is playing scrum-half on this occasion! To be honest, I don't have many problems. As they're assembling for a line-out, if I know it'll be shortened, I'll say: 'Watch your numbers!'

Derek: Another bit of preventative refereeing?

Ed: The last thing I want to have to do is count bodies. And if a line-out has formed but players start leaving it, first from one team, then from the other, I'll just stop the game and get them all back.

Derek: I heard you use a nice line in that situation. You said, 'Don't confuse me too much here, lads!' It made them realise what an untidy mess they were creating.

Ed: It *is* confusing. I might even say to the team throwing in: 'That line-out was formed – if you move away again I'll penalise *you*, and not the opposition.'

Injuries

Ed: Injuries . . . I'm probably the right guy to ask about them. For some strange reason I've been very unlucky with injuries while refereeing. Not so long ago I had fifteen stitches for an eye wound. Another time I broke a rib, or rather someone else broke it for me. Worst of all was when I wrecked the ligaments in my ankle.

Derek: Looking back, do you think the injuries were avoidable?

Ed: No. They were all freak accidents. Take the eye: I was refereeing Weston versus Birmingham, in very muddy conditions. As I ran across the pitch, a player in front of me – he was a massive guy – slipped and fell. I tried to avoid him and I slipped too. As I went down, his boot came up and a stud split my eyebrow.

Derek: You went off?

Ed: I managed to stay on, and they stitched me up afterwards. With the rib: I was refereeing Northampton against Harlequins. The pitch was perfect apart from one part that the sun couldn't reach, just in front of the sticks, and by Sod's Law that was where I had to be! A Northampton player made an attempted dropped goal. The ball hit an upright, came down and bounced on the crossbar; and I was stood underneath, looking up, waiting to see whether it fell in-goal or not. At that same time a Northampton centre, Rob McNaughton, came steaming up with his eye on the ball, too. He couldn't stop on the icy ground. We collided: bang, the rib was gone.

Derek: You went off?

Ed: No, I soldiered on. Maybe I should have gone off – that rib was very painful. The ankle ligaments were a lot worse. That was Midlands versus The North, also at Northampton – not a lucky ground for me! A scrum wheeled, and as I was moving away, a player stood on my foot, so the ankle was being asked to do the impossible, basically. Now that one really hurt. Did I stay on? I couldn't even stand up. Fortunately there was only a minute to go. Stretchered off, and home in a taxi.

Ed: This was the picture an instant before my rib got broken. A dropped goal attempt had hit an upright and then bounced off the crossbar, and I was watching it to see which side it came down. So was Rob McNaughton, the Northampton centre. The collision hurt me more than it hurt him!

Derek: I make it 114 miles.

Ed: Is it? Somebody else paid, I know that. The ligaments were in a real mess. If I'd broken the ankle, it would have healed quicker. As it was, I got help from Don Gatherer, then the RFU's honorary physiotherapist: brilliant. Even so, it was six months before I was refereeing, and eighteen months before the ankle fully recovered.

Derek: I'm sure most spectators – and a lot of players – don't realise how physical the game is for the referee. If he's going to be in the right place, he can't avoid getting knocked about.

Ed: Rugby today is not the game I remember from 1991, which was when I first came through to the international panel. The increase in fitness is phenomenal. Each season the game gets faster. Over the last couple of years I've noticed more and more top referees finding themselves in positions where suddenly they're having to get out of the way. I've had balls passed to me!

Derek: In top rugby?

Ed: Certainly, in top rugby. And that's an indicator of the pure speed of the game.

Derek: The ball won't hurt you – although I've stopped a few wild miskicks with my head, which makes your eyes water – but there are some very big guys hurtling around the field.

Ed: Big and getting bigger, and very fit and athletic as well. They're covering more ground and doing it faster.

Derek: This can come as a nasty shock to the novice referee, can't it? Say the line-out produces good ball, it's spun across the field, there's a tackle and a ruck. Our keen young referee gets there ahead of most players – and he stops. The next thing he knows, a flood of great hairy forwards is pounding past him, and he's getting knocked and shoved and banged and clipped on all sides.

Ed: Sounds familiar.

Derek: What can he do to protect himself?

Ed: He can get to the breakdown as early as possible. The sooner he can identify where the ball is, and decide which team is likely

Ed: Rugby gets faster every season – and one result is that referees get the ball passed to them! It's happened to me, even at the very highest level of the game. With rapid handling and sudden switches of direction, it's inevitable. The crowd blames the referee – but then, they always do!

to win it, the sooner he can move aside. If he positions himself on or about the offside line of the team which he reckons is going to win the ruck, he's cleared the route for all these late arrivals.

Derek: And if he can move to the *far* side of the ruck . . .

Ed: Even better. Wherever I stand, I'm side-on to these advancing players, not square-on looking at the ruck. So I make a narrower target.

Derek: Now all that works fine if you can identify where the ball is, and quickly. If not, you're going to be stuck in the path of the traffic. Bitter experience has taught me to brace myself, and prepare for the impact.

Ed: Again, it's often better to be standing side-on.

Derek: Occasionally you reach the ruck first, and stop, and a player who's running right behind you, doesn't. Wallop, right in the small of the back.

Ed: The reality is, they've got their priorities and we've got ours, and sometimes they clash. It's one of those areas where junior rugby can be a lot more difficult to referee than senior rugby. You can anticipate what senior players will do, but sometimes the junior players don't know themselves!

Derek: And I've got the scars to prove it.

Ed: If there's one universal criticism of referees at all levels, it's that we get drawn in a little bit too close, certainly at rucks and maul, often at scrums and line-outs too. Once we know where the ball is, we should back off, and maybe save our skins.

Derek: How much bigger and fitter and faster do you think players can get? I mean, some of them injure themselves just falling down. It may sound funny – but when you see these massive men travelling at such speeds, do you ever wonder whether the game was meant to be played like this?

Ed: It's a good question. Personally, I'm glad the International Rugby Board has tightened up the law about what players can and cannot wear. Because the hits have got harder, some teams – predominantly in the Southern Hemisphere – have been wearing shoulder pads or shoulder harness, or overgrown scrumcaps that are really halfway to being crash helmets, or reinforced corsets to absorb the tackle. But of course wearing equipment like that doesn't make the game safer. It makes it more violent. The hits are twice as hard, because players know they're wearing armour.

Derek: Sure. American football is the classic example. It developed from rugby, a hundred years ago.

Ed: If we're not to go down that road, we've got to draw a very clear line and enforce it *globally*. We've got to define exactly what you can wear – an unpadded jersey, unpadded shorts, jockstrap, T-shirt if it's cold, socks, boots, shinguards, mitts, shoulderpads, mouth guard. Chest pads for women players. Every item must conform to IRB Regulation 12. And if that protection isn't enough, you shouldn't be playing rugby.

Derek: Now, I agree with you that body armour distorts the game, but let's be reasonable about injuries. You wouldn't stop

Ed: Referees must expect to get knocked and bumped. Suppose the ball moves from one side of the field to the other. The referee moves fast. He stops near the point of breakdown to decide which team is winning possession – and a flood of players tears past him, sometimes through him. It's best to stand sideways (so you present a narrow target) and brace your legs. I also tuck my arms into my chest and hold my elbows where they'll protect me. And then hope for the best.

play every time a player goes down and looks unhappy, would you?

Ed: No.

Derek: He might just be winded.

Ed: He might have tripped over his own feet.

Derek: Or, of course, he might have dislocated an ankle. I've watched you referee when someone got badly hurt. You blew up like a flash, and you had the doctor on the field like lightning. Now, most of the time a rugby field is littered with bodies, and some of them get up very slowly. How can you pick out the real casualty?

Ed: There's a variety of telltale signs. Sometimes the players around him sort of half-stop: an instinctive reaction. Sometimes it's that horrible noise – a crack, or even a scream. Sometimes it's the way a player hits the ground – his body goes one way and his leg twists the other, and you just *know* he's not getting up. Or maybe two guys collide at such speed that someone's bound to be hurt. In the end I suppose it comes down to experience. You've seen so much rugby that you know instantly when it's just a knock and when it's really serious.

Derek: And if you think it's serious, you'll blow?

Ed: Immediately.

Derek: Really immediately? I mean, a team might be a couple of seconds away from scoring a try. That try might decide a championship.

Ed: I don't give a damn. At any level, from the bottom to the top, I'll stop the game the instant I see or hear a serious injury. I did it recently, in a Division One match, when one side had a brilliant scoring opportunity and two forwards had a clash of heads. I heard this terrible *crack* and I blew up straight away. Safety is absolutely paramount. Get medical treatment fast. One or two seconds might make all the difference. As I said to the guys at the time: 'That could have been you, laid out there.' Not that anybody had complained; they were concerned too.

Derek: I don't suppose you were sorry when the IRB banned the Flying Wedge and the Cavalry Charge at all age levels.

Ed: I was pleased. Those tactics caused too many injuries.

Derek: Inevitable, really, wasn't it? Defenders having to stand still while attackers charged at them.

Ed: I think medical opinion would say it's inherently dangerous. The player's safety comes first with me, and I'll even blow up if he's injured – maybe not seriously – and I think he's at risk of something worse. Suppose he's lying near a ruck or maul; somebody might drive off it and run all over him. I'd blow up before that could happen. Safety matters more than scoring or winning. Not everybody is in the professional rugby business. Some people have to go to work on Monday.

Derek: And there's something else to remember: litigation.

Ed: We live in a world of litigation. When someone gets hurt, the temptation is to look around and find someone to sue.

Derek: Preferably someone rich.

Ed: That lets me out!

Derek: But they might sue the appropriate Union *and* the referee. They might claim the referee was negligent in applying the law of the game, and that's why the guy got hurt. Then they might claim the Union was negligent in *allowing* this man to referee. That's how they hope to get at the big bucks.

Ed: You're right. Once the litigation lawyers get into the act, it's a nightmare. And it all goes to emphasise this point, that safety is paramount – and not just for the players' sake. I was very pleased when the IRB changed the law to let the physios on the field while play continued. For one thing, the referee might not have seen the guy go down, and for another thing, it gets attention to him fast.

Derek: Physios are good, but if it's serious, you want a doctor, don't you? What's your experience there?

HOW FIT IS THE DOCTOR?

Ed: At senior level, in the national leagues, a club *must* have a doctor at the game. I insist on meeting him in my dressing room. I want to know what he looks like and where he'll be sitting. I want to make quite clear to him what signal I'll give for him to come on: both arms straight up. When he sees that, I want him on like a shot. And – I mean no disrespect to the medical profession – if he's about 85, with a walking stick, he's no good to me.

Derek: He may need to run 70 or 80 yards across a muddy pitch.

Ed: I need someone who can react *quickly*. I also tell the doctor, 'If you think it's serious, or the physio does, don't wait for my signal. You're the expert – get on!' And I say to the physios, 'When you run on, if it looks serious, just holler!'

Derek: So the system works pretty well, does it?

Ed: It works pretty well until the unexpected happens. I refereed a match where a guy took a knock and had to go off to get a stitch. That was routine, but a couple of minutes later we had a really awful knee injury – and there was no procedure for getting the doctor out of the medical room. And that took valuable time.

Derek: You mean there's a case for having two doctors?

Ed: Yes. We only lost a minute, but a minute's a long time when the guy may be unconscious and nobody's sure why. At Bath rugby club, their medical back-up is excellent. There are *three* doctors at each game.

Derek: Nice work if you can get it. The reality for nine out of ten referees is a bucket of water and an old sponge.

Ed: You're right, and that's why, when you're refereeing at the lower levels, you've got to take even greater care. I'll stop the game – some people don't like this – if a player's stretched out and I don't know why because I didn't see the contact. He might just be knackered, or he might be unconscious. I'm not going to take a chance on that.

Derek: It's odd, isn't it, that when someone's injured, the teams usually go off and have a chat, and leave him to the referee. It annoys me sometimes. I'll tell the captain: 'Get over here. He's your player, he's your responsibility.' I want to know what the injury is, especially if there's a possibility of concussion, but I'm not going to treat the guy.

Ed: I sometimes see referees manipulating limbs and joints, and so on. I would never do that. Unless you're a trained, qualified medical man, you're running an awful risk.

Derek: Maybe I'm getting jumpy in my old age, but nowadays, unless I know the club's medical arrangements, I ask the coach or captain before the match: 'What's the procedure if we have a bad injury? Is there a qualified first-aider here? Where's the nearest telephone?' And as often as not, they give me a blank stare.

Ed: I think *all* referees, at *all* levels, should be asking that sort of question before the match. If the answer is that nobody with first-aid skills is present, then at least you know it and you don't waste time searching. If in doubt, send for an ambulance. My local club pays for a St. John's ambulance to be at all our home games. It costs us about £300 a year and it's repaid that cost ten times over. One of our guys had a dislocated knee – that's an awful injury – and the St. John's crew saved his career, through sheer prompt action and expertise. Marvellous.

Derek: You never answered my question about whether you wondered if the game was meant to be played so hard and so fast by such massive people.

SNAP, CRACKLE AND QUIT?

Ed: You've got to distinguish between senior and junior rugby. If you were to go into any dressing room before any international, and see the amount of strapping that the players apply to themselves, you'd realise just what a battering their bodies are taking. In the professional game, the lifespan of a top-level player is going to become shorter and shorter, I think. Not because of any illegality but because of the sheer ferocity of tackling and so on. We've almost reached the stage where these guys are *too* fit, and *too* fast!

Derek: Which might also explain why some international matches are very bruising to play and very boring to watch. Both sides are too good at knocking each other down. All penalties, no tries and the customer comes away feeling short-changed.

Ed: Well, the professional game obviously can't survive like that.

Derek: Which leaves the other 99% of rugby. Personally, I'm always amazed how few injuries there are. Thirty guys spend eighty minutes clattering into each other, and at the end they usually walk off more or less intact.

Ed: It's encouraging, isn't it? Shows we must be doing something right.

Offside

Derek: On paper, the law of offside in open play is very clear-cut, very strict. If a player's in front of a team-mate who kicks ahead, that player's liable to be penalised if he moves forward, even by half a pace. But is that the way the game is actually refereed?

Ed: No. It can't be. Unless you bring a sense of proportion to offside in open play, you'll be there all afternoon, blowing your whistle. Let's take an example: if a player's in a scrum that breaks up as the kick is made, he might quite naturally go forward a step or two.

Derek: It's instinctive.

Ed: Of course it is. In a situation where the ball's been kicked fifty metres downfield and a guy walks forward, if I say, 'Stop – you're offside' and he stops, I'm not going to penalise him. He hasn't interfered with play. But if he's halfway to where the ball's going to land and he's running forward – or even walking fast – I'm going to penalise him, because he's taking part in the game. If he doesn't distract an opponent waiting to catch the ball, he's bound to cut down his options just by coming forward.

Derek: He's offside *and* he's making a difference.

Ed: That's what matters.

Derek: This talking to players. You do a lot of it?

Ed: Yes. And if I say they're offside, I'm also going to tell them when they're *onside*. Teams are learning fast; at the kick-ahead they usually use their winger as the chaser to put their guys onside. If I don't say it, he will: 'You're onside, you're onside.' I don't have any great difficulty with this law, provided a player stops when I tell him to.

Derek: In that case, let's look at other kinds of offside. Many games are won and lost by penalties for offside. *Too* many.

Ed: It's frustrating for the crowd. It usually turns out that most of those offences are midfield offside at the set pieces: scrum, line-out, ruck, maul. If you're a No. 10 about to pass the ball to your centres, and you see the opposition sitting in their laps, the game is killed stone dead. Midfield offside is a curse on rugby. As referees, we've got to get the opposition back where they belong, onside.

Derek: How?

Ed: Let's take line-outs. At first-class level the other touch judge will position himself ten metres behind the line-out, so I ask that team's backs to use him as a guide. But whether or not I have the touch judges' help, I ask the No. 10s to be the leaders. In today's game, the No. 10 sets the alignment. The others stand where he wants them. When he breaks forward, they break forward. So I like to work with him. For instance, before the ball's thrown in, I might say to him, 'You're a bit too close – go eleven metres and that'll make up for the one you'll pinch in a moment.' That's the reality, and we both know it. What I also do, and so does every other referee in the world, is signal to the defending team's backs when they can move forward if – as often happens – the line-out develops into a maul. In law, the line-out doesn't end until *all* of that maul has moved beyond the line-of-touch – the imaginary line down the centre of the line-out. So my arm goes straight up as the ball is thrown and I might also shout 'Stay!' so they know they can't advance. If the ball leaves the line-out, or when all of the maul clears the line-out, my arm falls, the backs know line-out offside is finished, they're free to move.

Derek: Time was when the referee might warn the backs once against getting offside, and penalise them a second time.

Ed: True. Since arm signals arrived, they've reduced the number of penalty kicks considerably.

Derek: While they've given more responsibility to the referee.

Ed: Well, if I'm going to tell the backs to stay, it's only right and fair that I tell them when they can come forward.

Derek: In fact sometimes you actually wave them forward.

Ed: It's got to be a clear signal. All the stand-offs that I've refereed like it. They don't want to give away a penalty, but at the same time, judging midfield offside from a maul in the line-out – it can be a very subjective decision you're making.

Derek: Yes indeed. The backs are not ideally placed to know how far that maul has moved.

Ed: Exactly. When can they legally close down the opposition's space? I used to play stand-off, and there were times when I got it wrong both ways – gave away a penalty or hung back when I could have gone forward. As a referee, I'd sooner help the backs stay out of trouble than keep banging them with penalties.

Derek: Here's a funny thing. Thirty-odd years ago, referees were taught to use only three signals: try, kick and scrum. Now there are forty signals, all created by referees, all shown in the law-book – except for the line-out/maul/offside signal we've been talking about. Odd, isn't it?

Ed: Well, I've always believed the lawbook is the beginning, not the end.

Derek: Going back to penalties: most spectators would sooner see tries scored than goals kicked, but some people say there is still far too much offside and we should raise the value of the penalty goal to discourage offenders.

Ed: There's no easy answer. The International Rugby Board have a difficult job. They get told: 'Give the try a higher value and teams will want to score more tries.' My experience of rugby football is that players go out to *win*. They'd like to score tries, of course, but the first thing on their mind is *winning*. If you win the Rugby World Cup, even though the opposition scored four tries to one, you're not going to worry too much. In fact, it's been argued, and quite convincingly, that by putting the value of a try up to five points, we've encouraged players who are quite happy to give away three points for a penalty.

Derek: Just so long as they win.

Ed: We're moving into an era where the importance of results and financial gain is going to be bigger and bigger, and we're going to have more and more cynical people playing our game. That's going to make the referee's role a *lot* more difficult. There's a balance that we need to strike. If we referee to the laws of the game, and referee the same way for both sides, it can be a marvellous afternoon – provided everybody wants to play. Often it's the poor old referee who gets the blame for a disappointing match, when 99% of the time the *players* dictate the sort of game it is.

Derek: Leicester against Saracens in the Pilkington Cup. Two clubs with great talent, but on that day they didn't want to play rugby. Forty-four penalty kicks!

Ed: And it could have been twice that number. The referee did his best, but you can't control players who don't want to be controlled. But if the players have a positive attitude, and the referee gets the balance right, you can have a cracking game. I was lucky enough to see Harlequins play Bath – I was running touch – when both sides were totally positive. A fantastic game. If they won the ball, they used it. If they lost it, they tackled. Nobody was scampering around on the floor trying to kill the ball. Nobody was creeping offside. The referee could have sat in the stands.

Derek: If only we could bottle that spirit and sell it to all clubs.

Ed: The game would be much richer – and not just in money.

Advantage

Ed: I can't recall there being much advantage played by the referee when I was a player. And if there was, we didn't know about it, so he might as well not have bothered!

Derek: It's astonishing to think that the Advantage Law, as such, didn't exist until 1969. Until then, the Lawbook just had a paragraph about advantage, but it was so hidden and buried away, it obviously wasn't considered important.

Ed: Now it's one of the most valuable and creative aspects of the game. I can't imagine refereeing without it.

Derek: So what changed?

Ed: I think we all woke up. Players stopped expecting to hear the whistle for every little infringement. They started looking to benefit from their opponents' mistakes. And referees began thinking more and more about what the players were trying to do, and how to *use* advantage to help them.

Derek: The advantage signal has made a huge difference, hasn't it? Players see the arm shoot out and they *know* you've seen the offence, you're playing advantage, they feel encouraged to have a go. They've got confidence.

Ed: It's not just the signal. Certainly, in my case, I will shout: 'I'm playing advantage! Keep playing, keep playing!' Because a player stuck in a scrum or a maul won't necessarily see that the referee's arm is out. So the signal's just one form of communication. Advantage is very much a personal judgement. You'll never get two referees playing it exactly the same. It tells you a lot about a referee's personality, and especially about his confidence.

Derek: Why is that? After all, he can't go wrong, can he? If the advantage doesn't work out, he can always come back and start again. It's foolproof, isn't it?

Ed: No. It's not as easy as that; in fact, advantage is a very difficult area of the game. It can make a referee look good. It can also make him look very poor. If he isn't confident about his ability to control the game – and that includes having an air of confidence – then the idea of advantage should never even enter his mind. First he's got to have control and understanding. After that, he can afford to add the element of advantage, because he needs the confidence to know that if something doesn't work, he's quite happy to bring play back. And often it *won't* work. There are a lot of other factors that make a difference.

Derek: Such as what?

Ed: The temperature of the game. The attitude of the teams – positive or negative. The general atmosphere. Sometimes you can sense in the dressing room that everything's a bit too tense, too wound-up, and you think: *I've got to be really on top of this game or it might easily turn sour.* So there might be very little advantage played in the first ten minutes, because it's essential the players know you've got a firm grip on the game. When you feel confident that both teams really want to play rugby, you can begin to give them more opportunities to do so. Alternatively, the pre-match atmosphere may be quite relaxed, everyone's cheerful, it's a nice sunny day, and you could feel comfortable about playing advantage from the kick-off.

Derek: And sometimes the pre-match atmosphere is as tight as a drum – but they run out and surprise you.

Ed: Oh, it happens. Before the Neath–Fiji match everyone seemed tense, and I thought, *Hullo, this one's going to be a bit fierce.* In the first couple of minutes, Neath got the ball, it went fizzing out to the wing and I thought, *Blimey! They want to play!* I played advantage everywhere, even on the goal line. Both Neath and Fiji kept spinning the ball, and we had a cracking afternoon! So that worked out nicely. Other games begin well, everything's lovely for half an hour. Then suddenly there's a fracas, a bit of bad temper creeps in, you decide it's time to tighten the reins and get full control again. So – no advantage for a while. Keep it tight and formal. Remind them who's running the show.

Derek: Timing is everything, then.

Ed: And only experience tells you *when* to do it. Nobody can define that moment. It's very easy for an inexperienced referee to play so much advantage that all of a sudden the game's running him, and he's not running the game!

Derek: Yes. And he's probably too inexperienced to know it's happened.

Ed: He'll soon know if something goes wrong. Often I've seen games where the referee is trying to play advantage but the red mist has come down on some players, and that can develop into a dangerous situation, with one group of guys huddled together just knuckling one another while the ball's miles away. My advice to referees is always: get control first, then let the game expand – if the players want it.

Derek: Why wouldn't they want it?

WEATHER, SKILL AND OTHER VARIABLES

Ed: Well, I sometimes think we have a habit in the UK of almost *looking for a rest*. Very often you try and play advantage, and players on both sides have stopped! You realise they've had enough. So you come back for the offence and forget advantage for a while. Weather conditions have a great effect on advantage. *Great* effect.

Derek: Really? I'm surprised. I would reckon that in bad weather there are *more* mistakes, you play *more* advantage.

Ed: It depends. Some days, the weather is so miserable, the players are so wet and cold and numb, that they're just not alert enough to play advantage. And even when they are alert, you've always got to ask yourself: are the conditions favourable enough to *allow* the players to extract any advantage? Once in a while we all find ourselves in charge of a game where conditions are just farcical.

Derek: You took the Australia–Western Samoa game at Pontypool in the 1991 World Cup, and that was played in a monsoon, wasn't it? But you handled it so well that the video is still used to demonstrate wet-weather refereeing. There must have been a bit of advantage in there, surely.

Ed: Everything depends on the skill levels of the players. At Ponty those players were very skilled. At lower levels of the game, if you're up to the neck in mud, there's no point in just trudging on to gain a metre or two. Don't waste time giving advantage when it's obvious you're going to have to come back, anyway. If they haven't caught a ball all day, they never will! But even in the best conditions, it's the players' attitude that dictates how much advantage you can play. If they're more interested in carrying on their private duels, then say to them, 'If that's how you want to behave, as soon as an offence occurs, I'll blow it! And I'll blow for everything all afternoon.'

Derek: And would you say that at all levels? From international matches down to schoolboy games?

Ed: Exactly the same. At junior games I might make allowance for lesser skills. But if players aren't looking for advantage, then I won't give it. A referee needs some latitude to use advantage. If the game's quite fraught and tense and niggly, he hasn't got that latitude. Perhaps he'd *like* to play advantage, but he's not going to do it. He's going to tighten his grip and make everything very formal. The game has become too loose. He's got to create a tidy package again.

Derek: Everything comes back to confidence.

Ed: Yes. Your confidence in yourself, and their confidence in you. When you're both comfortable with each other, the sky's the limit. If two teams are just hell-bent on playing rugby, you can play advantage all day and all night because the lovely thing is if it doesn't work out, we can come back and start again. And players appreciate that.

Derek: It's all extra work for the referee, though, isn't it? First he has to decide whether or not to play advantage, and then he has to see what develops and judge whether or not the team actually got a real advantage. If yes, play goes on. If no, he has to remember what and where the offence was and bring everyone back for something which they've probably forgotten all about by now. Quite a lot to ask, that.

Ed: It just goes to emphasise what we've said before: the referee needs to have a real understanding of the game, a perception of what the players are trying to achieve. You've got to be aware of the players' strengths and weaknesses. It's no good going back to the halfway line and giving a penalty kick if nobody on that team can kick the ball more than ten metres!

Derek: Or if they're playing into the teeth of a howling gale.

Ed: Exactly. On the other hand, goal-kickers have had an amazing effect on advantage, because at the highest level you've got guys who can kick goals from the halfway line. Now, some people argue that, in those circumstances, after *any* penalty-kick offence in the opponents' half, the referee should *always* bring play back and let them kick at goal, unless they've gained a really worthwhile advantage.

Derek: And the referee is the man who decides what's worthwhile and what's not?

Ed: Yes.

Derek: Are you completely happy about that arrangement? It means the referee is looking at a passage of play and reaching a conclusion about what is right for that team – not legally, but tactically. The referee is wearing the captain's hat and saying, 'I'd sooner have this than that.' Why not give the choice to the captain? Surely he knows best.

Ed: Give me an example.

Derek: Well, suppose Blues knock-on. Advantage to Reds. They kick to touch and gain twenty yards. The referee might reckon that twenty yards is a sufficient advantage, whereas the captain might think that on a gusty, windy day the line-out's a lottery, and he'd sooner have the scrum, if you don't mind, sir.

Ed: It's an interesting point. In fact players are getting better all the time at using advantage and we need to be very aware of what they're thinking. But as to asking the captain where he thinks the advantage lies – that's a dangerous road to go down.

It would certainly complicate the game. It's our responsibility to decide, and we can't opt out of it. During a game I've heard the captain say, 'There's no advantage', and often I'll say, 'I'll decide if there's any advantage.' Because the captain won't always have the same view as the referee. And what he might not realise is there's a bit of niggle creeping in, a bit of friction, which makes the referee cut short the advantage so he can get full control of the situation.

THE NAAS BOTHA SCENARIO

Derek: Okay. But suppose a player says to you, 'Excuse me, sir, but I'm knackered and so are my lads. If it's a penalty to us, please don't play advantage. I don't want to run across the pitch and then have to come back. Just give us the kicks.' What's your response?

Ed: Oh, it often happens. Provided they do it in a courteous way, I think you need to listen and give them what they want. Sometimes they're not even knackered. They just say, 'If we get a penalty in our 22, don't try and play the advantage, please.' And if you forget, and you offer them advantage, they may simply apply the Naas Botha scenario.

Derek: How does that work?

Ed: It happened when I was refereeing a club game in South Africa in 1993. I signalled advantage from a ruck and the scrum-half whipped the ball out to Naas Botha at stand-off, and he just caught it and dropped it.

Derek: Vertically, I hope.

Ed: Oh, certainly. He dropped it because he didn't want the advantage. He went back for the penalty and kicked the ball 60 or 70 metres down the touch line. So, the bottom line is, if players don't want to take an advantage, they won't take it.

Derek: And of course, from a penalty to touch, Botha's team got the throw-in.

Ed: Exactly. That change in the law, giving the throw-in to the side awarded the penalty, has had an amazing effect on the way advantage works. It's one of the reasons why there are more penalties in games now. Referees are weighing up the situation and deeming that the greater benefit to the team is *not* to play advantage but to let them kick the ball into the corner. The team gets a good attacking line-out, on their ball. I remember a couple of incidents in the 1995 World Cup Final where I had to think of that sort of application of advantage. The first came from a New Zealand kick-off. It didn't go ten metres but South Africa accepted the kick, and this led to a maul where the New Zealand scrum-half was off-side. I didn't play advantage, because South Africa had little space to work in, and also the match had just begun and I wanted to be seen to be in control. Stransky took the penalty kick, and as it happened, he missed touch – but that's irrelevant; the point is, the way I read the game, an immediate penalty was what was needed. The second incident came later. There was a midfield ruck, again New Zealand went offside, but this time I played advantage. South Africa moved the ball and Stransky made a brilliant kick that found touch a few yards from the New Zealand goal line, but of course it was a New Zealand throw-in. Now I would have been within my rights to bring play back to midfield and give South Africa a penalty. The crowd wouldn't have liked it. It would have been poor entertainment. On the other hand, South Africa might have kicked the goal. I didn't give the penalty. The South African players had no complaints about that. But it was a very difficult decision.

Derek: And what's more, you've got just one second to make it. Here's another point about advantage: the referee knows when he's playing it, and half the players may know – but the other half may not. In all the noise and confusion, the referee's signals may be lost, so the players might assume, 'He missed it – he's having an off day – right, we'll take over!'

Ed: That's exactly right. And it's why – and I keep on saying this, because it's absolutely crucial – confidence comes first. They've got to be able to trust you to get it right, and you've got to be able to trust them to do their share. Your confidence is paramount. It takes confidence to turn advantage on, *and* it takes confidence to turn it off when you see that it's doing more harm than good. Advantage follows control. No control – no advantage.

Ed: You can't tell a team what it wants. You can offer them advantage, but equally they can decline it. This happened to me in South Africa, in a match where Naas Botha was at No. 10. His team won good ruck ball although an opponent was well offside. I played advantage. The scrum-half passed to Botha and he deliberately knocked the ball down. He wanted the penalty kick. I blew up, penalised the offside, and Botha kicked the ball sixty metres to touch.

Derek: But you are willing to accept a certain degree of contribution from the captain?

Ed: Oh, certainly. If I've got an advantage completely wrong – which can happen – there's nothing wrong with a polite request from the captain, such as: 'If that situation happens again, please just blow up and give us the kick.' All he's doing is helping the referee's thought-process about how they want to play the game.

Derek: What's your experience of playing advantage in the Southern Hemisphere?

Ed: They'll take it to the extreme. Partly that's because handling conditions are better, but mainly it's instinctive. They know they're in the entertainment business. That means keeping the ball in play, so that's the way they're refereed in their part of the world and that's what they expect from us. I'm quite sure in the Northern Hemisphere our expansion of advantage will get wider as we realise we're in the entertainment business too.

Derek: There's a downside to advantage, isn't there? Once you've signalled that you're playing advantage, you've told the world about it – and if you get it wrong, if you blow up just when the attack looks good, then the groan is pretty deafening.

Ed: It's a very frustrating mistake, and we're all guilty of it at some time. Who knows why? Maybe something catches our eye, makes us look away, some off-the-ball incident, and we're thinking of two things instead of one. It shouldn't happen but it does. That's why it's much easier to play advantage when the only thing the players are interested in is the ball.

Derek: Right. Now, as far as the young referee is concerned, if there's one thing more difficult than knowing when to play advantage, it's knowing when to stop playing it, when to quit. You see referees running up and down the field with one arm stuck out, and very uncomfortable it looks. So what's your advice?

Ed: Well, it all depends.

Derek: I was afraid of that.

Ed: It depends on the referee's individual judgement of the situation, and *that* will depend on what *type* of offence you're playing the advantage from. Is it from a minor infringement, such as a knock-on? Or is it from a middle-range offence, like off-side? Or is it from something much more serious – foul play, a high tackle, for instance?

ADVANTAGE FROM FOUL PLAY

Derek: Let's start with the last. Let's say a centre is high-tackled, but he gets his pass away and you play advantage.

Ed: The only way I would *not* bring the players back and award a penalty kick would be if a try was scored or the advantage gained was pretty massive. Even then I would speak to the guilty player and I might even caution him or send him off. But in general, foul play cannot be ignored. Unless the advantage leads either to a try or to a large and considerable gain, I'm going to give the kick every time. Simple as that.

Derek: Well, let's try and tighten the focus on that. Suppose the centre gets high-tackled when he's in front of his posts, and his team uses the advantage to run the ball up the field until they're stopped in front of the opposition's posts. Are you going to bring them back and give them the penalty kick?

Ed: No.

Derek: Not even if the high tackle was really vicious?

Ed: If it was, I'd have blown up at once, so the question wouldn't arise. In the situation you described, they moved the ball virtually the length of the field. That's a really hefty advantage to them. Better than a kick inside their own twenty-two.

Derek: Even though they knocked-on in front of the opposition's posts, so the team that committed the high tackle gets the put-in at the scrum?

Ed: Yes, I think so. The team that used the advantage had their chance, they gained a great chunk of territory, that's good enough. If they knock-on, they take the consequences. That doesn't mean the player who made the high tackle gets away scot-free. If I think he deserves a caution, he'll get one.

Derek: Okay. Same scenario, but the team using the advantage get stopped on the halfway line, where they knock-on. Do you bring them back and give them the kick?

Ed: I might. It's a matter for the referee's judgement. What are the playing conditions? What are the skill levels? What's the weather like? They've gained forty-plus metres – well, in some circumstances that might be considered a really big advantage, in other circumstances it might not.

Derek: Especially as the opposition would get the put-in.

Ed: That's a factor.

Derek: Suppose they *wouldn't* get the put-in. Suppose the team taking the advantage got stopped on the halfway line and a ruck formed. Nothing came of it. They were going forward, so you know they're entitled to the put-in if there's a scrum. Does that affect your decision?

Ed: It might. The law governing the penalty kick to touch is very important here. If a team couldn't run the ball out of their own half, and if I thought they had a kicker who could hoof it into touch in their opponents' half and keep the throw-in, I might well go back for the kick. Lacking a good kicker, they might be better off with the put-in at a scrum in midfield. But nobody can lay down hard-and-fast rules. You weigh up the game on the day, and decide accordingly.

Derek: All right. Now, when it's a penalty-kick offence but *not* foul play, how do you treat it?

Ed: Offside is what comes to mind. Again, the set-up on the field has a big bearing on the referee's thinking here. Suppose Reds are playing Blues. If Reds are attacking, in front of the posts, and a Blue player comes offside, I'll play advantage if I can. And if Reds' attack fails, I'll give them the chance to kick the points. Or run the tapped penalty, if they wish.

Derek: And does that apply no matter how long the Reds' attack takes? They might switch play from wing to wing, and back again? They might win half a dozen rucks?

Ed: If they couldn't score a try, I'd always give them the kick. In this situation, close to the opponents' goal line, the advantage is a score. If they don't score, you give them the kick.

Derek: Now let's shift play to Reds' half of the field. Blues go offside, and Reds break out and run rings around the Blues and finally get stopped deep inside Blues' half.

Ed: How deep?

Derek: On the 22.

Ed: I might well consider that Reds had gained sufficient advantage.

Derek: You would forget the offside?

Ed: I would probably have a word with the guy who'd been offside. I wouldn't penalise him. It comes down to this: what damage has he done, and what advantage is available to his opponents? If he's offside near his own goal line, he's probably shutting down the other team's options for attack. Their only advantage is scoring – they can't make much territorial gain. Whereas if he's offside in his opponents' half, they've got great scope for territorial gain.

Derek: In between those two extremes, of course, is a large area of the field where the place-kickers can make hay.

Ed: Exactly. The modern game has bred these guys who can kick 50 or 60 metres to touch, or kick at goal from almost anywhere in the opposition half – or even outside it. That's a set-up we've got to be aware of, because basically what we're trying to do is use advantage to let a team play as it wants to.

Derek: And what about playing advantage from a free-kick offence?

Ed: I'm trying to think of a situation . . . Mostly, when a free kick's awarded they just tap it and run.

Derek: Suppose you saw foot-up by a hooker but his opponents won the heel against the head?

Ed: Oh, I'd definitely play advantage there. And unless they made a right pig's ear of their possession, or their scrum was being driven backwards, I wouldn't come back for the kick.

Derek: So you're not going to be too generous when it's only a free-kick offence.

Ed: Well, I'm happy to give the opposition the chance to profit from it, if they can. But if the offence is nothing to get excited about, I'm not going to stop the game – unless I've got to.

ADVANTAGE FROM TECHNICALITIES

Derek: Okay. Now we get down to the real bread-and-butter stuff. Knock-ons and forward passes.

Ed: Technicalities, rather than offences.

Derek: Sure. Let's assume, for the sake of argument, a knock-on happens on the 15-metre line. The blind side is a bit cramped, but the open side is wide open. The opposition snap up the ball.

Ed: Advantage means getting only one bite of the cherry. What I'm looking for is good speed and good space. Here, I'd play advantage because Whites have knocked-on, straight into the hands of a Black player – so that's good speed. And Blacks have plenty of room to turn this quick possession into attack, so that's good space. Speed and space add up to opportunity. For me, that's enough advantage. If Blacks cock-up their opportunity, I won't bring play back and give them the scrum for White's knock-on. Blacks don't deserve two bites at the cherry.

Ed: If they win good possession, and if they've got space and time to use the ball, then I would suggest that they're in a stronger position than if I blow up and give them the scrum. So I'll play advantage. The fact is, the existence of that space and time has already *given* them an advantage.

Derek: Let's take it further. From the knock-on the ball gets fed back, passed across-field, an attack develops and suddenly it's checked. What's going through your mind now?

Ed: Speed of delivery. That's the first thing I look for. If they get the ball quickly and they've got space to work into, I would actually tell them: 'You've had your advantage.'

Derek: You count the *opportunity* to attack as an advantage. Right?

Ed: What more can they want? They've had time and space. You've given them all the advantage in the world. Now it's 'Over to you. You *take* advantage of this opportunity.'

Ed: The situation here is similar to the last illustration – a White player knocks-on and Blacks get the ball. Again, I'd play advantage. But Blacks have neither good speed nor good space. The ball is bobbling about on the ground, so the Black player will lose time just getting hold of it. He has support waiting outside him, but his team-mates are closely marked by the White defence, so the space is not good. Blacks' opportunity is poor. Maybe they'll gain from the advantage (a Black player might chip over the defence, for instance) but if they don't, I'll bring play back and give them the scrum.

Derek: Okay. The same set-up but the full back comes into the line and gets tackled. Knocked flat. Only ten yards from the original knock-on. You're still not going to blow up?

Ed: No, I don't think so. The only time I'll blow up and give them the scrum is when – for whatever reason – they've had slow ball or no space to work into, or both. But if this lot have had quick ball and good space, then as far as I'm concerned, they've had all the advantage they're entitled to.

Derek: Even if they make no territorial gain at all?

Ed: Advantage one way can breed advantage the opposite way. Here's an example. First there's a knock-on by Whites. I play advantage to Blacks, who have good speed and space. They run the ball across the field. This gives them their bite at the cherry. Now Blacks knock-on, and the ball goes straight to a White player. I play advantage to Whites, and provided they too have good speed and space I'll let the game go on. In fact there's no reason why I couldn't play advantage back to Blacks for a second time in this same sequence. If play became too loose and sloppy, I might decide that enough is enough, but otherwise I'm happy to play all the advantage there is.

Ed: That's right. Of course you'd like to see them make territorial gain, but what we've got here is the 'two bites at the cherry' syndrome. They can't expect to be given a large opportunity to do something useful, and then make nothing of it *and* be given a scrum as a sort of consolation prize. That's two bites at the cherry, and it's one too many.

Derek: Yes, I can see that. But how can you say a team has enjoyed – for want of a better word – advantage, when they've ended up no better off?

Ed: Because they've been allowed the opportunity to make themselves better off, and that in itself is the advantage. A lot of people think that advantage must mean territory, but that's not so. If somebody knocks-on and you get the ball away *quickly* to where you've got *time* and *space,* you've had quite an advantage! *Quite* an advantage. And if you then drop a pass, I would be loath to bring play back and say, 'Scrum down, lads – you've gained no advantage', when I know in actual fact that they have!

Derek: Fair enough. Now, let's take the scenario one stage further. Knock-on, ball quickly won and moved out, fullback into the line, and *he* knocks-on. Do you play a second phase of advantage?

Ed: Oh, yes. I would play advantage to the other team. Provided their control is good, there's not piles of bodies on the floor, the package is tidy – yes, I'd play advantage back the other way, to try and keep the ball alive, keep people playing.

Derek: So . . . according to that philosophy, there's really no limit to the amount of advantage you could allow in one sequence of play.

Ed: That's right. Provided the players have got the right attitude and enough skill and know-how, there is no limit. You can go on and on. The only change comes when you're looking at possible penalty kicks. Then you have to weigh up a lot of factors – position on the field, type of game, skill level of kickers, the Naas Botha scenario, and so on.

Derek: Let's just look at the Naas Botha scenario again. He deliberately dropped the ball in order to take the penalty kick. In effect, he was declining advantage. Suppose a similar thing happened from a minor offence?

Ed: You mean, suppose someone knocks-on, and I signal advantage, and the stand-off takes a pass and deliberately drops the ball.

Derek: Yes. Would you blow up and give that team the scrum?

Ed: I would. On the same principle.

Derek: Well, in that case, it's very important for the team who are gaining advantage to know what's happened, isn't it? Was it a knock-on or was it offside? Are they in line for a scrum or a penalty kick? It makes a difference, doesn't it? If it's the first, and they run with the ball and cock it up, they won't even get the scrum. Whereas if it's the second, they know they can afford to take a risk because they can't lose. So what do you signal? When it's a penalty-kick offence, does your arm go up high to signal penalty kick, and then down to the horizontal for advantage?

Ed: No, it doesn't. My arm goes straight out and I say, 'I'm playing advantage.' Often the guys in the backs have a better view than me; they know exactly what's happened. If the ball's come away quickly and there's an offside, I'll call out, for instance: 'Playing advantage – 12 Blue offside.'

SHOW THEM AND TELL THEM

Derek: Can they hear you? In a big stadium, with all the crowd noise?

Ed: I really shout it. All the time I'm telling the players, 'I'm still looking for advantage – keep going, I'm still looking for it.'

Derek: Rough on the vocal chords, isn't it?

Ed: I'm often hoarse by the end. Some people say we ought to shut up and leave it to the players, but I think that if we can help them to play advantage to the full, we should do it.

Derek: Clubs are always saying it would be a damn sight easier to play everything to the full if referees were more consistent. As you yourself said: advantage is very much a personal judgement. No two referees play it the same.

Ed: It must be frustrating, sometimes.

Derek: The players are always having to adjust to a new referee.

Ed: I was at a conference where one of the coaches asked the referees if we could make advantage more uniform. I said that that would be impossible, because every game is slightly different, and every referee's understanding of the game situation is slightly different. The great beauty of advantage is its total flexibility.

Derek: Yes, but the players aren't in any doubt about what they're trying to do, are they? They practise very hard to achieve it. Why can't referees adjust to what the players do? Maybe referees would referee better if they spent more time with clubs on their training nights.

Ed: I've argued that for years.

Derek: We're always complaining that players never bother to learn the laws, but they can equally say that we pay no attention to how they play the game. Ref pops up on Saturday afternoon, that's the first time they see him.

Ed: Exactly. As referees, we stop playing, we disappear from the playing side, we sometimes become a little bit indifferent to what the players are trying to achieve.

Derek: And *how* they're trying to achieve it.

Ed: I've been involved with the Bristol club for years now. I would train for an hour with one or two players who are coming back from injury, maybe referee a contact session, and maybe answer their questions. The great thing for me is just to *watch*. Particularly their work on the scrummaging machine. Just watch, and listen to the props and the coaches, and build up a sort of global understanding of their game.

Derek: And maybe learn a lot of stuff you never suspected before.

Ed: Exactly. If you look at the RFU coaching exams, they have a section that is pure law. Coaches must pass this section. If you look at a referee's exam, there's nothing whatsoever about coaching or understanding the game. There should be a bit in *both*. We don't want textbook robotic referees. We want referees who actually understand the game. Because if the players know that you've got empathy – not sympathy, but empathy – with their game, then they'll take you into their confidence. They won't take into their confidence a referee who's just a Textbook Charlie.

Derek: And confidence is the key to playing advantage.

Ed: Which is where we came in!

Miked-Up

Ed: At the top level, one man can't referee a game now. Those days are over. You need the help and support of your touch judges. You need a Team of Three.

Derek: I had a touch judge once. Nineteen-sixty-five, I think it was.

Ed: You don't need to tell me how difficult it can be to referee a junior game, out in the back of beyond, and it certainly does any international panellist no harm to experience that again, and remind himself what rugby's all about. I take a 3rd XV match from time to time.

Derek: Perhaps the lawmakers should go along and watch, just to remind themselves how 99% of all rugby is played.

Ed: Perhaps they should, because that's the big problem, isn't it? One Lawbook is trying to contain two different games. The game at the highest level is not played the same as it is elsewhere. It's a different game completely.

Derek: In that case, is it refereed differently too?

Ed: Yes. I couldn't referee an international the same way I referee, say, a Wednesday school game. For a start, I need my touch judges to form a Team of Three, because top-level matches are played at such a cracking pace, the pressure is so terrific, and the big decisions are so crucial, that the back-up of touch judges – top referees themselves, remember – is crucial. A couple of years ago I took the Harlequins–Northampton game when the result meant that one club or the other got relegated, and relegation meant that club losing a million pounds a season, so

I'd better do a good job, hadn't I? In those circumstances I welcome all the help I can get.

Derek: Totally understandable. And in fact you get more help than the laws allow, so it looks as if the Lawbook isn't big enough to contain both games.

Ed: Strictly speaking, the duties of a qualified touch judge are to signal when and where the ball is out of play, report incidents of foul play, and assist the referee with kicks at goal.

Derek: Foul Play. That's a long law.

Ed: Anything a player does that's against the letter and spirit of the Laws of the Game is Foul Play: obstruction, unfair play (time-wasting, for example), repeated infringement, dangerous play, and misconduct, including any act contrary to good sportsmanship. And it applies anywhere in the playing enclosure. Very comprehensive. Before the match, the referee would brief his touch judges about which areas of Foul Play he wants them to flag – maybe obstruction, for example – and which he wants them to communicate by other means.

Derek: If your touch judge is going to flag obstruction, he might as well flag off-side. And a deliberate knock-on. Or maybe *all* knock-ons. I mean, why not?

Ed: Because now it's getting too complicated. I don't want all that information, and in any case touch judges are not always best placed to make those decisions. For example, it might look like a knock-on to a touch judge fifty yards away, but I can see the ball went through the guy's hands and came off his chest. The referee's got to remain the man who makes the decisions. His touch judges are there to help him out in a few vital areas – not flood him with information he doesn't need and can't absorb.

Derek: Okay. So what do you want?

EXTRA EYES

Ed: I want the same as the players and coaches – a fair shout. I want the right judgement to be made at the right time. As I've said before, players don't demand perfection. They accept that we all make mistakes occasionally. What they *won't* accept is that, for example, a try has been wrongly awarded (or *not* awarded) just because in law it says the touch judge can intervene for one thing but not the other – and in this instance it was the other thing that made all the difference. Now, I agree that we're only talking about experienced, qualified, neutral touch judges and they are the minority. In the vast majority of games, the referee's got to shoulder the burden himself. But at the senior level I believe the lawmakers need to expand the role of touch judges.

Derek: Fair enough. So tell us what you ask of them.

Ed: I want their eyes and their experience. The referee can only look in one direction. If something happens that I miss, I hope my touch judges will see it. I want them to take a wide view of the game, and not just follow the ball all the time. If there's dangerous play I want them to flag it, even if they *know* I've seen it. We don't need to meet and confer every time – I can give him a nod or a wave, and he knows I've got it covered. That's why touch judges' experience is so important. For instance, suppose there's a high tackle. I'll almost certainly see it, but I might play advantage from it. The touch judge has to be smart enough to realise that. Touch-judging is hard work. You've got to be thinking like the referee all the time.

Derek: Let's assume that while you're haring off, playing advantage, the player who got high-tackled gets up and starts putting his boot into the guy who did it. All behind your back.

Ed: Yes – and I'd want my touch judge to flag that, and keep flagging it. He's my extra pair of eyes. And when we meet up, I'd want a very brief report from him.

Derek: Suppose you miss a knock-on.

Ed: Let's face it, we all miss knock-ons. A game of rugby can get very congested. No matter how brilliant your positioning is, players suddenly twist and turn, bodies obscure your view – you've missed it, and your instinct and the players' reaction tells you so. If the touch judge has seen it, he can let the referee know. Why put phenomenal, pressure on ourselves when we can use a little commonsense?

Derek: And then there's offside. Not at rucks and stuff, but midfield.

Ed: Well, we've talked about that. 'A blight on the game' is what the International Rugby Board calls it. Question is: how do we correct it? We need to use more than one person; we need to use the Team of Three. For instance, at a line-out, the touch judge on the opposite touch line stands ten metres nearer the defending team's goal line, so he's marking the offside line for that team's backs. Now they've got no excuse for standing offside. If my touch judges are constantly monitoring the midfield offside, it's amazing how well-behaved the backs become. Which is one less problem for me.

Derek: And what's more, thanks to the miracle of micro-technology, you're miked-up nowadays, all three of you. I've got mixed feelings about this. On the one hand, it widens the gap between the game at the top and the rest of us. On the other hand, if you've got a Team of Three they obviously need to communicate. I suppose I'm jealous, really.

Ed: The system works well. The referee wears a small transceiver clipped to the back of his shorts, an earpiece, and a button mike that's always open so his touch judges can hear every word. The touch judge wears an earpiece and a button mike which is not always open – he has a push-to-talk button that lets him communicate with the referee. All very simple, and so lightweight you forget it's there.

Derek: What's a typical message?

Ed: A touch judge might say: 'Blue number twelve, midfield offside now.' That's plenty. It's got to be very, very brief. I've got enough to concentrate on without someone rabbiting away in my left ear. If he intervenes six times in a game, that's enough. A dozen times is far too many and twenty is impossible.

Derek: Plus, of course, there's two of him.

Ed: Exactly. And he's *advising* me, not *instructing* me. If a centre's offside at a scrum but the opposing scrum-half chips and chases up the blind side, I'll play advantage.

Derek: Players can see the mike and the ear-piece. They know what's going on.

Ed: Often they'll ask me before the match: are you going to be miked-up? It's had an amazing effect, as a deterrent. Not just against midfield offside – at rucks and mauls, too. The fringes are much cleaner because players stay back an extra half a metre. Scrum-halves find they have more space to work in. They like miked-up games, very much.

Derek: Now, the 1991 Rugby World Cup was the first time you were regularly miked-up for the benefit of TV and radio commentators, wasn't it? That has to be a good idea.

FIELD EARS

Ed: Yes. I first came across it when I did the Tests in South Africa in 1993. They went further: introduced Field Ears, head-phones which let spectators hear the referee's comments, a magnificent idea, so it's no surprise that it spread. In the UK it's at Twickenham, Cardiff, Murrayfield. Called Ref Link – like listening to an iPod. People feel closer to the game, they under-stand it better. Fantastic.

Derek: It must open up a new dimension. I've played a video of a match you refereed, and the soundtrack is only your voice, your comments, plus the odd player's voice. It made me realise that what I *saw* was only half the story

Ed: In the modern game, the referee's live-to-air in virtually all broadcast matches. All part of marketing the game, educating the audience.

Derek: How do you feel about that?

Ed: I'm all for it. I think it's a really positive innovation, because it helps the spectator to understand the referee's calls: what his decision was and why he made it. Usually it shows the referee in a positive light, which makes a nice change! There is a possible downside. If the referee talks too much, the public might get bored. However, vocal referees like England's Tony Spreadbury are popular with the listeners. His bubbly personality comes across loud and clear. My family and friends get a kick out of Tony's handling of the game.

Derek: There's rugby law, and there's litigation. I can picture a situation where a guy gets badly hurt, and the lawyers pick through the referee's remarks, and quote him and say, 'You knew this was happening; why didn't you take action to prevent it?'

Ed: You're right. Miked-up and Field Ears and so on are magnificent systems, but we need to sort out the legal snags.

Derek: Now that the Team of Three is miked-up, why not include the touch judges' contributions in Field Ears?

Ed: I think that's dangerous. On the field, the referee has to be sole judge of fact and of law. If a touch judge says that No. 12 is offside, and the referee disagrees, and everyone on Field Ears hears them . . .

Derek: It's not good for the game.

Ed: You've got it.

Derek: Anything else about the Team of Three you want to throw in?

Ed: Yes. I was in France in 1995, running touch for Brian Campsall in a match between New Zealand and a French Provincial side. New Zealand scored, right in the corner. The scorer took a Frenchman with him. Brian awarded the try and walked away, towards where the conversion kick would be taken. For some reason, something made me wait, and not run to the posts. As the New Zealand player got up, the French player lashed out and kicked the tendons at the back of his ankle. I flagged it immediately, New Zealand converted the try, Brian cautioned the French player, award a penalty on the halfway line, and New Zealand kicked the goal.

Derek: Ten points.

Ed: Nobody saw the foul except me, until we all went to the aftermatch function. They replayed the match on a big screen, and when it happened, everyone went, 'Ooooh!' So my point is, it's very easy for officials to relax once a try's scored. And incidentally, I'm not convinced that we position ourselves best, as touch judges, when the try's scored in the corner. We usually run slightly behind the players to see if the ball-carrier puts a foot in touch or hits the corner flag – but if he's tackled, there are bodies between us and the ball. Maybe we can't confirm that he grounded it. In Australia, the touch judge positions himself on the touch-in-goal line, which means all the action is coming *towards* him. He can still see the touch line and corner flag and he's got a much clearer view of the try. But wherever he positions himself, he should never relax after the score. Don't turn away. As long as there are bodies on the floor, there's still a potential problem.

Derek: The referee's concentrated all his attention on the big question: did he score? Having got *that* terrific decision out of the way . . .

Ed: Momentarily, he relaxes! We all do it. I'm as guilty as anybody. We turn away.

Derek: And that's when a defender arrives and lands hard, with his knees or elbows, on the scorer.

Ed: The try's been scored but the action hasn't ended. So why is the touch judge racing to the posts? There's no hurry. He should wait and watch out for trouble. If the referee isn't working with a Team of Three, he himself should wait and make sure that no foul play follows the score. It's easy to turn away and miss the defender who arrives too late to do anything except knee the scorer in the back.

Ed: If you talk to Rory Underwood, he's got strong views on this. He says that we have not refereed this area very well at all, and I think he's right. We've been too lax. The defender knows that he's too late to prevent the score, but he dives on the scorer anyway and bangs his knees in the guy's back.

Derek: He's thinking: *I can't stop him, but I'll hurt him.*

Ed: Exactly. Hurt him, slow him down. It's a professional foul, it's dangerous play, and we've got to learn to look for it. We can't relax because the try's scored. We can't relax *ever*, until the final whistle.

Rucks and Mauls

Ed: One of the biggest developments in the game – and in the laws of the game – is the arrival of the ruck and maul. I mean, they are now units of play in their own right, which they never used to be. When I began playing, rucks were called loose scrums, and when did mauls get properly identified?

Derek: There was no law of ruck or maul in 1949. They must have been added in the next twenty years. I know they existed in 1969, because that was when I worked on a rewrite of the Lawbook.

Ed: 1969! You've been around a long time, Derek.

Derek: The secret is regular breathing in and out. It certainly kept me going through long years of refereeing, down there in the grassroots. Not brilliantly, but better than nobody.

Ed: Exactly. And it's a privilege to be asked to referee a match at *any* level of the game . . . About rucks and mauls: they need to be refereed well, because that's where teams hope to win quick possession before the opposition can reorganise. So it's a part of the game where the referee must concentrate very hard.

Derek: Now, you talk about keeping the game tidy. That's impossible at rucks and mauls, isn't it? By definition they are always going to be *un*tidy.

Ed: We as referees can do a lot to keep them from becoming a complete mess. We can stop players fringing – hanging about on the edges, where they're offside. We can stop players joining the ruck or maul at the side; if they always join from the end, alongside their hindmost player, we get a much tidier shape. We can penalise guys who try to collapse a ruck or maul, and so on.

But after that, it's up to the players' technique. If they haven't got the skills to work the ball back, make it available, it's going to end up trapped inside. But if the referee knows where it is – even if he can't see it – and he decides there's a good possibility it's coming out, he should give that team every chance to use it.

Derek: Yes . . . Some might say he gives them every chance, and a bit more. The law says a player in a ruck can't handle a ball, it's got to be won with the foot. But if the scrum-half sees the ball in the ruck, and he reaches in and drags it out, the referee looks on and smiles.

Ed: Maybe he doesn't smile. He certainly hopes the guy won't drop the ball.

Derek: But if a great hairy forward in the middle of the ruck does the same thing, he gets penalised.

Ed: Probably. If he's seen.

Derek: So referees have decided to give the scrum-half immunity from the law about handling in the ruck.

Ed: In effect, yes. What you describe is quite prevalent in the game today. We do allow the scrum-half to go into the ruck and *burrow* slightly for the ball.

Derek: Up to his wrists? Elbows? Armpits?

Ed: Normally he won't see the ball unless it's quite close to the edge of the ruck. And then what we're trying to do is get the ball away, and away more quickly. As far as the scrum-half is concerned, we're treating him much the same at rucks as at mauls. The law has always let him burrow into a maul and rip the ball free. Well, now we're letting him do the same at rucks. And of course, once he's dragged the ball out and he's got it in his hands, the opposition can grab him. He's fair game.

Derek: All the same, it does mean he's been given a sort of favoured status, doesn't it? Which is not in the law.

Ed: Some people might argue that we're being over-sympathetic to that scrum-half. All the time, the pressure is coming from this need to entertain. Now the England coaches have said that if a

Ed: If the ball is nearly out of the ruck and the scrum-half burrows in for it, I won't penalise him for handling in the ruck. His team has clearly won the ball, and it just needs a hand to help it exit the last few inches. That's allowable. The ruck's won and lost; let's get the ball out and away as fast as possible.

team has obviously *won* a ruck-ball, we should allow players in the ruck to push it back by hand.

Derek: Known as 'hand-rucking.'

Ed: Yes. Again, the aim is to get the ball away more quickly. As referees we end up walking a very fine tightrope. It's always difficult when you find yourself having to say, 'Okay, we know the law and we know we're going *against* the law – but that's what we're going to do, because . . .'

Derek: Because, in the case of the ruck, the team has *earned* this possession?

Ed: They've earned it. Their opponents have no hope of winning it. So let's do the business as quickly as possible.

Derek: Yes. Or, in the case of some scrum-halves, as slowly as possible. You often see the ball lying in the open at the back of the ruck for several seconds, while the scrum-half looks around and decides where to pass. Or you see the ball being held for him to take, totally outside the maul, while he has a good look around. The ruck's over. The maul's over. But heaven help any opponent who comes around and takes the ball. Ten to one the referee will hammer him.

Ed: Teams don't recycle the ball fast enough, I grant you that. They can be very grudging about releasing it, and then very slow to use it once it's released. Beats me why.

Derek: The faster the better, I would have thought.

Ed: When I refereed Bath versus Northampton there was a classic case. Northampton won a ruck and the ball came back out. I mean, it was well clear of the hindmost feet. I was standing on Bath's offside line but wide of the ruck, so I had a nice angle to see everything. Matt Dawson was scrum-half. His hands were on the ball for one second, two seconds—

Derek: Just holding. Not passing.

Ed: Ben Clarke, Bath's No. 8, saw this. Ben had been onside. He knew the ruck was over, knew it was open play, and he tackled Dawson. Took him, man and ball. Jamie Salmon was commentating on TV, and his exact words were: 'I can't understand how the referee failed to see the offside.'

Derek: Obviously Jamie didn't know his law – but to be charitable to him, maybe he'd seen a lot of referees who had penalised the tackler in the same situation.

Ed: I wouldn't be surprised. I was at an RFU session for the National Referee Development Squad, where they showed lots of snippets of tape. When Ben tackled Matt, everyone looked at me and said, 'What's the problem?' And I said, 'No problem!' The scrum-half can't have it both ways. Once the ball's out of the ruck, he's fair game.

Derek: Yes. But the very fact that you discussed it suggests that some referees are giving the scrum-half total protection – almost unlimited freedom to use the ball.

Ed: And that can't be right.

Derek: Before we move on from the ruck/maul situation, just consider this set-up. Reds are playing Blues. Reds kick off. A Blue player catches, his teammates form a wedge around him. Familiar picture, right? It's not a maul.

Ed: You see this all the time. From a kick-off, a White player catches the ball and teammates bind on him to create . . . what? Not a maul. A maul must include at least one opponent. Usually some Black players arrive and obligingly form the maul. What if they don't? What if they follow the arrow to the back of the wedge and grab the ball? They can't be offside. There's no maul, so there's no maul offside line. Personally, I'm quite glad when the maul forms, it's much tidier. But it's not compulsory. If Black players go around the wedge and poach the ball, the crowd get very upset – but the crowd is wrong!

Ed: No. A maul would need at least one Red player bound on.

Derek: So there's no maul offside line.

Ed: Correct.

Derek: So any Red player can legally go right around that Blue wedge and grab the ball.

Ed: It's open play. He can go where he likes.

Derek: He'd be a bit brave to do it, wouldn't he?

Ed: More than a bit. This ploy came up at a training session at the Bristol club. They asked me to comment, and I said, 'To be honest with you, you're probably better off not going around there.' Because I know the opposition would just drag the guy out by his head – and then an even bigger problem would arise! So . . . maybe the answer is that sometimes it's best not to encourage the players to know too much! [LAUGHTER] But the reality is that there's no maul, and if someone's cute enough to go around and get in that hole, he can make himself a nuisance! It looks awful, though, doesn't it? And people find that difficult to understand.

Lines of Running

Derek: You seem never to get caught out of position. That must be all about your lines of running. Explain to me the secret.

Ed: Anticipation.

Derek: Yes. Is that all?

Ed: Well, and fitness, I suppose.

Derek: Nothing more?

Ed: A little bit of luck.

Derek: You see, I was hoping we could have a whole series of illustrations showing your lines of running, with dotted lines and bent arrows and stuff . . .

Ed: Can you illustrate anticipation?

Derek: I don't think so.

Ed: Lines of running, angles of running, they're all part of positioning. Nobody has ever told me about positioning. Nobody. Your instinct tells you. Anticipation.

Derek: This is going to be a very short chapter!

Ed: Well, it's a very quick decision, isn't it? You see what's happening and you just *go*, and get there as fast as you can. That's how everyone referees: they look, anticipate, go.

Derek: All at once.

Ed: There's no time to hang around, is there? And what makes the best referees just that little bit better than the good ones, in my opinion, is that they are slightly better anticipators. I like to see referees who've played quite a bit of rugby, who understand what the game's about. Their instinct tells them what's likely to happen next and how to get there.

Derek: There's a bit more to it than that, though. Plenty of times I've done everything you said, and then got barged sideways by a player who had his own personal lines of running.

Ed: And never saw you.

Derek: Well, let's give him the benefit of the doubt on that.

Ed: It's important to make your angle of running so that you're not going to interfere with anybody. They won't forgive you if you get in their way – they might miss a tackle or not take a pass, because you slowed them. That can be very frustrating. But equally, I sometimes find players cutting across *my* line of running when I'm in full flight, and I've got to check. Once they've slowed me up, I'm dead, especially if the ball's gone wide and I need to get to the corner. That's my biggest worry. For whatever reason, my line of running suddenly gets cut off, I'm forced to check, I've probably lost ten yards. I may shout, 'Get out of the way!' but the reality is, the game's so fast now, I'll never catch up.

Derek: I've seen players run the *wrong* way – *away* from the ball – and make the referee dodge or stop.

Ed: Oh, certainly. They've committed themselves in advance. The ball goes elsewhere, but they stick to Plan A! You've got to be ready for anything.

Derek: So the fact is that lines of running are not just a simple matter of anticipation and speed. You've got to avoid spoiling the lines of running of players who are faster than you. You've got to avoid being checked by players who are slower than you. And it's a good idea not to get flattened by some joker who's moving in completely the wrong direction.

Ed: And that's happened to me too.

Derek: So the reality is, the referee's going to have to weave his way across the field?

Ed: Sometimes. Not often. At the highest level of rugby, the ball and the players move so quickly that there's normally space to work in. It's not often that I'll be in front of, say, the No. 7. If the ball's been won cleanly from the top of the line-out, I might just be ahead of a couple of props and a hooker. Everyone else already has 15 or 20 yards advantage on me. That leaves space for my line of running.

Derek: I've just remembered something else. While the referee is belting across the field, he can't actually look where he's going. He's got to watch the ball – and that may be off at a considerable angle from his line of running.

Ed: It pays to have panoramic vision. Or so I'm told.

Derek: But then – and this has happened to me hundreds of times – while you're running one way and looking the other, you sense these ghostly shadows at the edge of your vision, about to cut across your path, so you take a quick glance – and that's when a player knocks-on, and you missed it.

Ed: Well, that's called self-preservation, and there's nothing wrong with that! But you're right: the referee can't relax for an instant. He's got to think hard and run hard. All the same, his first decision is based on pure anticipation. His feeling for the game says: *Go there*, and he goes.

BAD LINES OF RUNNING

Derek: That's all well and good, but it's not a tremendous help to the young referee who keeps finding himself in the *wrong* place. So let's approach it from a different tack. What's the sign of a bad line of running?

Ed: When you can't see the ball. That's got to be number one. New referees are so accustomed to playing that sometimes they can't resist following the ball. They get far too close, they keep having to dodge, and their view is obscured by players. It pays to keep your distance. The next bad sign is not keeping up with play. That may be part and parcel of the first fault, because the referee often finds himself running in an arc instead of a straight line. When he anticipates rightly, he cuts the corner – he runs to where the ball *will be* and not to where it *is*. So he's well positioned to see the forward pass, or scissoring, or whatever. Most new referees get far too close to the action, and that affects their lines of running as well. But even if they get the line right, that won't help them if they're not fit. Players are getting faster all the time.

Derek: I don't see how referees can get any faster. Not at the top level, anyway.

Ed: By the time someone's acquired the experience to be a senior referee, he's not going to be a spring chicken. I'm coming in contact with players who are twenty years younger than me. There's no way I'm going to be as fast as they are, so the only way I can beat them to a situation is by anticipation in my lines of running. One disadvantage of being at the front of the line-out is that I've got a lot of ground to make up. I just accept that. But I never *stand still* anywhere, I'm always *moving* as the hooker throws in. It's hard to run from a standstill. Much easier if you're already moving. That's true everywhere.

Derek: One of the first things a new referee learns about positioning, especially at the line-out, is not to stand between the scrum-half and his fly-half!

Ed: They'll soon let you know. Maybe the scrum-half wants to get the ball back to his full-back. You've got to give them clear passage.

Derek: And rucks and mauls? Where do you position yourself?

Ed: Once I know which team is likely to win the ball, I'll try to stand on their off-side line but a few yards to one side of the ruck or maul. I want to see the ball *and* the opposition perhaps fringing or coming over the top *and* make sure their backs stay onside – but at the same time, it's important not to block the line of running for any player who may be standing off the ruck or maul. I mean, he knows where he wants to go if he gets the ball, and he might say, 'Move out of the way, ref.' More often I'll say, 'If I'm in your way, just nudge me.'

Derek: That's a lot better than getting knocked sideways. These big guys can move fast.

Ed: Keep moving. A referee should never be static. If you're at a standstill it takes valuable seconds to get off the mark. If you're already walking or jogging it's easy to accelerate into a sprint. As the ball is thrown in to the line-out, I always move forward. Within seconds I'll be running hard. I've got to be ready or I'll be left behind.

Ed: And one of my criticisms of referees is that we tend to get drawn in too close, at rucks and mauls. Here's an example: I was refereeing Munster versus Swansea, and I got into a hole alongside a maul. Two Munster men were standing off from the maul. I expected the first man to take a pass and charge forward. Instead, the scrum-half missed him out and passed to the second guy. I was blocked, I couldn't get out of the hole. He drove

Ed: *After I've reached the point of breakdown – in this case a ruck – and identified the ball, I move fast to that team's offside line. This gets me out of the way of arriving players. From here I can see the ball, and watch out for fringing players, and keep the opposition behind their offside line until the ball's out.*

forward – he was a prop – and the front of his head hit the back of mine. He went off with a split eyebrow, I had a nice big lump. All because I got my positioning slightly wrong.

Derek: Did you blow up when he hit you?

Ed: No. He knocked me flat, of course, and as I fell, my only thought was: *Did I obstruct the Swansea defenders?* I decided not. Munster scored. They got five points and their prop got six stitches. And I learned a lesson! Referees who've retired are inclined to say that that sort of thing never happened in their day, and they're probably right – but the sheer *speed* of play is so different now. Referees are getting bundled over more often, and I think we'll see it happen even more in future. So my advice to referees is: Get some medical insurance!

Derek: And some tetanus jabs.

Ed: Oh, certainly.

KICKS AT GOAL

Derek: Let's talk about positioning for kicks at goal. It's another area where you've got to think of the player, isn't it? Things like not letting your shadow fall on or near the ball. He starts his run, the referee moves, his shadow distracts the kicker.

Ed: Exactly. Some people think a kick at goal is a chance to have a rest. You can't relax. Certainly, in the '95 World Cup I had a problem.

Derek: Which game?

Ed: France–Ireland, in Durban. The sun was causing havoc for the touch judges behind one goal. The kick was from wide out. The sun was behind me, so I wasn't sure what the problem was, but there was a long, long, long delay before the flags went up! Afterwards the guys told me that they were looking straight into the sun and they both lost sight of the ball. Now, if they couldn't

Ed: Positioning for kicks at goal is important. At a conversion kick I stand slightly behind the kicker and between him and the touch line. That way I don't distract him, and I'm looking straight up the path of the ball, so I'm well placed to see if the kick is successful. The ball will go dead, so I needn't worry about the follow-up action.

Ed: Positioning for a penalty kick at goal is based on the fact that the ball can still be alive after the kick, and so it's essential to be near it when it comes down. I stand in front of the posts, level with the kicker (but always far enough away that I don't distract him). When he begins his kick, I start to run. Anything can happen. You've got to be there to see it.

see, I would have had to make the decision. As it happened, I was happy that the kick had gone over. But it underlines the point: you can never relax.

Derek: Where were you standing for that kick?

Ed: It was a conversion kick, so I was standing on the kicker's blind side, near the touch line. For a penalty kick at goal I stand centrally.

Derek: Why the difference? They're both kicks at goal.

Ed: Yes, but I know the ball's going to go dead after the conversion kick, so I can afford to concentrate on the path of the ball. The ideal place to follow the path of the ball is from where it was kicked – that gives you the best opportunity of seeing if the kick is good or bad. If I haven't got touch judges, I'll make a header for the posts. Whereas with penalty kicks, the ball is still alive if the kick fails, so I want to be in midfield where I'm close to the action, if there is any.

Derek: And if the French are playing, there probably will be.

Ed: If the ball goes into the French in-goal, just don't assume *anything*. Just because the kick at goal has missed, don't assume they'll ground the ball. They can be up and away and on the attack. Even if the kick ends up at the rear of the in-goal, watch it! Watch the ball all the time. Never prejudge any situation, never relax, always be prepared for the worst – them moving out, and you having to be on your bike!

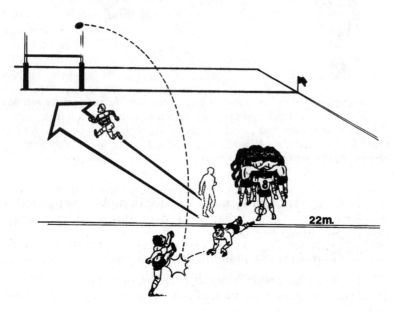

Ed: Positioning for a dropped goal attempt is very simple. You go to the posts as fast as you possibly can! Ideally, you want to be under the crossbar, looking up at the ball. Realistically, you hope to be near enough to the posts to know whether or not the kick is good. Anticipation helps. The illustration shows South Africa's winning dropped goal in extra time of the 1995 World Cup Final. Stransky's body-attitude told me he was going to drop for goal, and I was sprinting to the posts while his kick was on its way. Fortunately, I had a good view of it going over!

Derek: And there's the other possibility: the kick bounces back off the posts and the winger's in for a try.

Ed: You've got to be there. It's unforgivable if you miss it.

Derek: What's even worse is if you give a try when it never was. Even when the attacker's got the ball behind the posts, it can all go horribly wrong, can't it? Richard Harding, the England scrum-half, actually punched the ball out of a French winger's hands when he was behind the England posts! Half a second later and the try would have been scored. Many a referee would have relaxed when he saw the French winger run around behind the posts.

Ed: Lots of times I've seen an attacking player cross the goal line and just . . . drop the ball. It happens when he's under pressure but it also happens when no defender is near him. He's done the hard work, he's made the line, and he relaxes. The ball just falls out of his hands. It happens more and more these days with guys doing these lovely swallow dives – and losing the ball in the process. Well, the player can relax, that's up to him, but we can't. Until the ball is grounded, we can't take anything for granted. There's always the possibility of something silly happening, and the in-goal is *the* most important area. You've really got to be working, not only to get there but when you're in there too.

Derek: There can't be many tougher decisions than two guys diving on a rolling ball that's inches short of the dead-ball line.

Ed: The dreaded kick-and-chase. Remember the incident in the '91 Rugby World Cup? Wales versus Western Samoa? Kick deep into the in-goal, the referee following on, players ahead of him, both diving, both claiming the first touch.

Derek: Samoa got the try and won the match.

Ed: A very difficult decision to make. But we live and die as referees on those decisions; that's the reality.

Derek: If there's one kick at goal on which your reputation might have lived or died, it must have been the dropped goal that won the Rugby World Cup Final for South Africa in 1995.

Ed: I thought it was actually going to go wide, at one point. It was high, so that wasn't going to be a problem, but the way Stransky connected with it, he was bringing it in from right to left, and it just *swerved* towards the middle. Now you imagine if I'd got it wrong!

Derek: It's unthinkable, so I'm not even going to think about it. Simple question: you see the guy shape to drop for goal. Where do you go?

Ed: There's only one place you *do* go. That's between the sticks. As straight and as fast as you can. If you can't see, then you can't give. You've just got to *be* there. And the only way to do that is by anticipation. In the Final, I knew Stransky was going to drop that goal. Even before the scrum, I had a pretty good idea that he might have a go. The moment he received the ball I saw his body position and I *knew* I had to run!

Derek: That scrum was on the twenty-two, wasn't it? You had to run quite a way to the posts. And it was towards the end of extra time – so all the fitness training paid off. I suppose the height of the kick helped . . .

Ed: A high kick gives you more time, but on the other hand a high kick may fall just under or just over the crossbar. I was in the United States in 1990 to take their Inter-Collegiate Final, and there was a massive dropped-goal attempt from the half-way. I tore after it and got close enough to decide it just went over. The spectators disagreed! And it was even more dramatic at Northampton, when the ball fell on the crossbar and actually wobbled before it made up its mind which way to fall. The referee's got to be underneath that one.

Derek: One of the more rewarding aspects of refereeing is to read the player's mind and be at the posts as the drop-kick goes over.

Ed: Yes. To be honest, the kick that you can anticipate isn't much of a sweat, usually. It's the kick you're not expecting that might catch you out. Zinzan Brooke's dropped goal against England in the '95 semi-final – I don't think Stevie Hilditch could ever have anticipated *that*.

Derek: Zinzan Brooke was on the wing, wasn't he? On the England 10-metre line?

Ed: And he just let fly. An incredible kick, right out of the blue. And it just emphasises what I keep saying: you can't relax for a second.

Roots

Derek: You and I have some things in common. We both grew up on council estates in Bristol. I grew up in Sea Mills and read too many books and became a novelist. You grew up in Hartcliffe and read a lot of books about rugby and —

Ed: And became an electrician.

Derek: Yes. But you also became probably the best referee in the world. I know many players who would say *the* best.

Ed: I've been lucky.

Derek: We've both been lucky. We've both worked hard at what we're naturally good at, and made ourselves better, but timing is everything in this world and I think we were lucky to be born at the right time. I wrote my books just when people wanted to read that sort of stuff. You came on the rugby scene just when players wanted your sort of refereeing.

Ed: A lot of truth in that. The changes that revolutionised modern rugby actually began about fifteen or twenty years ago.

Derek: So if you'd been born in 1942 instead of 1952, the rugby establishment might not have been ready for your refereeing. You might never have made it to the top. Timing is everything.

Ed: The referees of the old school were a bit formal, a bit distant. No doubt that was what the game wanted then. I'm not saying they weren't good – some were brilliant. But I wouldn't have been comfortable doing that. In any case, the game changed and referees changed with it. I wasn't the only one, far from it. Just in the Five Nations alone, when I took up the whistle we had John West and David Burnett in Ireland, Ken Rowlands and Clive

Norling in Wales, Alan Hosie in Scotland, Mike Titcomb in England, Francois Palmade in France – all outstanding referees. And I could name a dozen more, outside Europe. I just carried on the good work.

BAPTISM OF FIRE

Derek: Sure. But – in the words of that bloody awful song, you did it your way. I'm thinking of your very first international, France against Scotland. You stretched the elastic quite a lot on that day, didn't you?

Ed: I played advantage every chance I got, right from the kick-off. Both teams wanted to play open rugby, and I gave them all the help I could. When I came off, Ken Pattinson, who was the international assessor that day, was three feet off the ground. 'That's not how you referee your first international!' he said. 'You play little or no advantage for the first twenty minutes! *Then* you open it up . . .' He was quite upset.

Derek: Well, it's understandable. His way had worked for him.

Ed: I did what I felt comfortable with. The players liked it. Some good rugby got played that day. I certainly enjoyed it. That's the way I'd always refereed, and I saw no reason to change it for an international.

Derek: As a world-class referee you're somewhat unusual, aren't you? I mean, you're not in one of the professions. I've met international referees who were headmasters, senior R.A.F. officers, lawyers, high-ranking policemen, university lecturers and so on. You grew up in Hartcliffe, which is a tower block estate with a fairly tough reputation. Let's start at square one. Where are the Morrisons from?

Ed: Ireland, originally. My mother came from Tipperary to be a trainee nurse in England, and she met my father in Bristol. He was from Belfast. A builder's labourer. I don't remember much about him: he died when I was eight. I remember plenty about my mother – she's very much alive, I see her every week – because she brought up all six of us on her own. Very strong woman. Tough as nails.

Derek: Sounds like she had to be.

Ed: That's true. I remember she forced me to stay home from Hartcliffe school, once, because I was sick, and so I missed three days. Those were the only days I missed in five years. School was the best time of my life, I loved it, I can't understand anyone who doesn't like school. Hartcliffe was huge, one of the biggest comprehensives in the West of England, so we had excellent sports sides. I was mad keen on sport – soccer, cricket, rugby, basketball, tennis, athletics, I did them all. Revelled in it.

Academically I did no work. I was too busy enjoying myself. I learned nothing. During the '91 World Cup, Fred Howard and I visited an Edinburgh school. They asked us where we'd been educated. Fred said Hull University, I said Hartcliffe University – I could see the kids wondering: where the hell's *that*? The truth is, I left school a complete failure. What you said is absolutely right: I'm a hobbledehoy, compared with these professional guys.

Derek: Well . . . nobody's a *complete* failure. There must have been *something* you were good at, besides sport.

Ed: The one thing I was good at was leading. Even when I was quite young, I was house captain and so on. Unfortunately it didn't last. I wanted to stay on, in the Sixth Form. They said: why? I said: because I'm having such a good time! They said: but you're not learning anything! So I got thrown out at sixteen, because I wouldn't do any work.

Derek: So now you *had* to work, whether you liked it or not.

Ed: I did a five-year apprenticeship as an electrician, and then I joined what's now British Aerospace. Spent 21 years there – from the shop floor to cost control to electrical estimating – until 1994. The firm had always been very good to me about time off for rugby, but I could see that times were changing and I took voluntary redundancy.

Derek: So when you refereed the '95 World Cup Final, you were actually on the dole.

Ed: Quite true. It wasn't easy to combine the demands of rugby with steady employment. The greater the demands, the harder it got. Luckily the RFU offered me a job in their refereeing department and that's where I've been ever since. But the game has brought me rewards that can't be bought with money. I've got rugby friends all over the world.

Derek: Good referees – I've heard you say this – need to have played a bit. You played more than a bit.

Ed: I did. Rugby was a love of mine from the start. I went from hooker to wing forward to stand-off. That was the position I played for the Bristol Boys team. Then I had a couple of years with Hartcliffe Old Boys RFC until it folded and finally I joined Bristol Harlequins, which is a perfectly typical junior club. You'll find hundreds, if not thousands, just like it, scattered all over the country, and I think they're the backbone of the game. Quins ran five teams. I was club captain for four years. We won the Bristol Combination knock-out cup – out of about fifty clubs in the area – so we weren't bad, were we? I had some good mates who were playing senior rugby, and they were generous in passing on their views and knowledge. And I read a lot about rugby when I was young.

Derek: Now that's unusual.

Ed: So I've been told. Mainly autobiographies. Gareth Edwards, Barry John. What made them tick, an insight into their level of effort.

Derek: Okay. If we just freeze-frame somewhere in the 1970s, what we see is a conventional figure: a guy in his twenties, electrician with British Aerospace, with a wife and three children and a hobby. To be honest, there's not the slightest sign of anything extraordinary, is there?

Ed: None at all. The only unusual part of me was my knees. They took a bit of a bashing and I had an operation. Give it up, the doctor said.

Derek: And being an intelligent, mature, responsible maniac you went out and played some more.

Ed: And broke various other bits. Finally – it was the first game of the season, we were playing away, and I forgot to put my kit in the car.

Derek: Freud would have had something to say about that.

Ed: I'm sure! Anyway, I scrounged some kit, and within three minutes of the kick-off, I broke my jaw.

Derek: Forget Freud. Someone up there was trying to tell you something.

Ed: Fate. I was wired-up for six weeks and living on a liquid diet, and I decided it was time to bale out while the rest of me was in one piece. I joined the Bristol Referees Society.

KEEPING IT SIMPLE

Derek: First match you took – I looked it up – was Old Bristolians 3rd XV versus North Bristol 3rd XV, on 5 September 1982. Remember it?

Ed: Nice sunny afternoon. Most of the players knew me from being captain of Quins, they weren't too concerned. Within a few moments they became confident in me as a referee. Of course I got things wrong, let things happen that shouldn't. But I did one thing right. Before the game I went to an old friend and very good referee, Mike Morgan, and I said, 'How do you go about refereeing the game?' Mike said, 'Referee it as you think it should be played.' That advice was invaluable. And he also said, 'If it looks wrong, penalise it; if it looks right, leave it.' Very simplistic, of course, but it worked for a beginner. So my refereeing was completely naive, held together by an understanding of what I believed the game was about.

Derek: Which was what?

Ed: Win the ball and let's see it moving around! That's the atmosphere I've always tried to create – from that day to this.

Derek: I've checked the records. You were a slow starter: you spent two years as a probationer referee, twice as long as most people. Didn't you begin to feel a bit stifled?

Ed: No.

Derek: No ambitions?

Ed: None.

Derek: I'm baffled. How can you reach the top without being ambitious?

Ed: I didn't set out to reach the top.

Derek: So what did you . . .

Ed: For the first few years I just went in, refereed the game, had a few beers – and went! I never applied any pressure to myself. My attitude was, 'Right – I enjoyed playing but that's finished, now I'll do some refereeing. I'll enjoy that too, and if people like it, I'll move forward, and if they don't – well, that's tough!' Whereas I think we're now producing an animal that decides from an early age to become an international referee – and if it doesn't materialise, he goes off and plays golf. We're recruiting more referees than ever before, but the problem is that we're losing so many.

Derek: They start with big ambitions, and throw in the towel.

Ed: Yes. But it's not a disaster if you don't make it to the top, is it? The game has got to be serviced at all levels, not just at the very highest level, where it's played only by a very tiny minority. Take our town: if we don't put out a hundred referees every week, then we're not covering all the games. That's important. International referees get the kudos, but they only do a very small part of the job.

Derek: Your first years of refereeing were pretty relaxed, then.

Ed: Totally relaxed. Totally laid-back. I used to turn up in a T-shirt and jeans. Then Mike Morgan saw me like this, and he said to my wife, 'Lin, for God's sake get him tidied-up.' Which she did. Collar and tie and stuff. And all the time, of course, I was getting tremendous help and guidance from the experienced guys in the Bristol Society. They got me better games, with bigger clubs.

IN AND OUT THE COMFORT ZONE

Derek: Still no ambition?

Ed: My sole aim was to go out and enjoy myself.

Derek: Just an interesting pastime.

Ed: Exactly. One reason I kept that attitude was because I went up the ladder so quickly, I had no time to think differently. I began refereeing in 1982. In 1987 I went on the 'A' list, in 1988 on the RFU list, in 1989-90 on the international panel.

Derek: Well, *something* must have happened in those years. I mean, you don't mature as a referee by taking easy 3rd XV games on sunny September afternoons.

Ed: No, you don't. The system of refereeing is basically that you should build up your experience within the comfort zone – inside your Society, your city or county or whatever. And so you increase your confidence, and your reputation. It's just like being a player; there's a lot of word-of-mouth. Teams know you, so they're comfortable with you. That strengthens your confidence.

Derek: And then all of a sudden the Society sends you outside your comfort zone.

Ed: In my case it was near Northampton, to do Kettering versus Ipswich 2nd XV. This was the big test. They didn't know me, I didn't know them. All I had was what I took with me: my values, my understanding of the game, my confidence in all of that, my confidence that 'This is the way the game should be played'. And it was enough.

Derek: It sounds like you took some of your comfort zone with you.

Ed: Yes. Some referees can, some can't.

Derek: Can't travel?

Ed: I know an excellent referee, greatly respected locally, whose confidence evaporates when he leaves that comfort zone. He's very comfortable with people he knows, but put him with people he doesn't know and his personality changes.

Derek: Are you saying that in every referee's career there might be a point where he reaches his ceiling, maybe bumps his head on it, and if the bruise is bad enough, down he comes?

Ed: Down he comes to his particular level, I would hope. It's the level he's most comfortable at. We need people who are good at every level. They're absolutely essential.

Derek: What about you? In the years when you went rocketing upwards, did you ever bump your head and wonder what the hell you'd hit?

FROM RUSSIA WITH NO LOVE

Ed: Oh, yes. The first national team I refereed was when Combined Services played Russia. Within two minutes I knew I was going to have big problems with the Russians. Their perception of the game was the opposite of mine. I'd never before come up against a team that was totally oblivious to anything and everything I said and did. That was a massive stage in the learning curve.

Derek: Did they speak any English?

Ed: Some did, but they didn't want to use it.

Derek: And foul play?

Ed: Very little. The obstacle was just their complete refusal to go along with the referee's decision-making. A refusal to retire ten metres, a refusal not to shove before the ball was put in, a refusal to do anything I wanted!

Derek: Sounds like a grim afternoon.

Ed: It was probably the most difficult game I've ever had to referee. It's one of those occasions when you just dig in and you grind it out for eighty minutes. Every referee meets one eventually, and he's just got to grind it out. He's got to remember that he has the ultimate weapon. The players have lots of things but they haven't got the whistle. Games like that are no fun, but they're good experience. They're useful to get under your belt.

Derek: What did you learn from it?

Ed: Several things. I learned that it's a mistake to referee two big games on consecutive days! I did the first-ever Under-21 Varsity match on the Tuesday morning and then the Combined Services–Russian game on Wednesday evening. That's too much. I wasn't fully prepared, mentally, for the second game. I learned what a big difference the weather can make. It was December, conditions were really foul, biting wind, bitterly cold. I remember I had to almost drag the Russians out of their dressing-room. Then we all lined up for the anthems.

Derek: I've heard the Russian anthem. Keeps threatening to end, but never does!

Ed: It went on and on and on. While it was being played, we had a sleet storm. Everyone was frozen. I can remember thinking: *What am I doing here?* The Russians certainly didn't want to be there. I learned a lot, that night. I learned that maybe this refereeing business isn't quite so easy, after all! I refereed Russia again, a couple of years later, against Combined London Old Boys. Nice warm evening, the pitch was in marvellous condition, no wind, and both sides just played rugby. It was a lovely game.

Derek: Can you honestly say you enjoyed that first game?

Ed: I enjoyed the challenge. At every level, some games are going to be all toil and no laughs, but if you can rise to the challenge and get out in one piece, there's a sense of achievement. Refereeing is about facing the challenge. It doesn't always go right for you, and when it goes wrong, that's not too enjoyable. It's like falling off a horse: you've got to jump back on again. The day you have a bad game, try and get another game, soon. Get the failure out of your system. Get your confidence back.

Derek: When you were climbing the ladder, who were your role models?

Ed: Nobody.

Derek: You never went to a big match and watched the referee?

Ed: Never. I can't do it. Doesn't interest me. I watch the players! Much more interesting. I've never looked at a referee and thought: *That's the way I'll do it.* Whatever works for the individual is right. Never imitate. Do what's comfortable for you, what's natural.

Derek: That's an interesting word, 'natural'. Did you find that all your refereeing came naturally?

Ed: No. I had to work very hard on several areas. Signalling advantage was one – it never came naturally to me. In the beginning, sometimes I signalled and sometimes I didn't – which is almost worse than not doing it at all. I used to shout, 'Playing advantage!' but that's not enough, not everyone hears you, you must signal as well. It wasn't an instinctive action for me. I really worked at it.

Derek: Was that one of the things the assessors criticised you for? I know you got watched more and more closely.

THE HYPERGOLIC REFEREE

Ed: I owe a great debt to assessors. Every game I took, there was an intelligent, perceptive report on my performance. I was able to improve in areas where I never suspected I wasn't up to scratch. Alan Welsby, who's a former international referee, wrote some tremendously helpful reports.

Derek: I've seen some. He didn't spare you, did he?

Ed: He had things to say about almost every aspect of my game. One was the way I signalled penalties. He thought it could be improved.

Derek: Here's what he wrote. 'You immediately flicked up your hand and arm in a "hypergolic" manner, such that many an Olympic gymnast would have been proud of the degree of convexity that you were able to achieve from the spinal curve.' And he added: 'Unfortunately that is not what we are about.'

Ed: Alan was right. I was getting a bit theatrical. Mind you, I had to ask him what 'hypergolic' meant.

Derek: His next report says it means 'exploding or igniting spontaneously'. Your signals must have been worth the price of admission alone.

Ed: I remember he gave me a lot of stick – quite rightly – because I confused people when I awarded penalty kicks and free kicks. Sometimes I blew up, raised the arm and immediately swivelled so that the arm pointed the opposite way! That sort of irritating little mistake can ruin a referee's career. Alan's report coached me in the correct procedure. He didn't just find fault, he was very positive, very constructive.

Derek: In fact, his final advice was to go out and practise on your own, on an empty pitch.

Ed: Which I did. I ran about, imagined an infringement, blew up and practised the correct signal. I must have looked daft to anyone out walking his dog, but it's little details that decide whether or not you get on the international panel.

Derek: In seven years you went from the grassroots to the international panel. I can't believe that didn't change your outlook.

Ed: It did. I thought: *I quite like this!* And I began taking it all seriously. Up to that point, I took the eighty minutes seriously, but not the rest of the game.

Derek: What's so important about the rest?

Ed: Everything's important. It matters how you dress, how you behave, how you're perceived as an individual. When you're an international panellist, you're more than a referee – you're a representative of your Union, of your country. It means presenting yourself properly: haircut, shave, tie, blazer, crease in the slacks, shine on the shoes. Or, to put it another way, if you're seen dead drunk in the gutter, you won't be on the International panel for long!

Communication

Ed: Well, I think it's been the biggest revolution in the game.

Derek: Even bigger than the arrival of professionalism?

Ed: Far more wide-ranging than that. Let's face it, the open game has directly affected only a tiny handful of players. How many get paid? Fewer than one in a thousand. But the simple fact that referees now *talk* to players, and *listen* to players, and *communicate* in order to create a better game for everyone – that's a revolution. It's transformed rugby in the last ten or fifteen years. Everything's different.

Derek: You may find it hard to believe this, but in 1964 I wrote a little 40-page booklet for Americans called *Rugger: How to play the game.*

Ed: Funny how soccer is still called soccer, but the word 'rugger' has gone right out of fashion.

Derek: Well, maybe I helped kill it off. One of the things I wrote was: *Remember that the referee is not obliged to tell you what your offence was, and that you have no right to ask.*

Ed: Good God. That was in the laws?

Derek: It was. What's more, my booklet got reprinted by Twickenham and by the New Zealand Rugby Union.

Ed: In the Seventies, when I was playing, the referee was a sort of god-like figure. He blew his whistle and said 'Kick' or 'Scrum' or whatever, and if we understood why, that was nice, and if we didn't, well, that was nice too. The reality was, nobody argued – well, hardly anybody – but half the team didn't understand.

Derek: And didn't *expect* to understand. There seems to be a tradition in rugby that the players don't understand the laws of the game.

Ed: They almost take a pride in it.

Derek: You can't imagine any other sport where the players make such a tremendous effort on the field, but as soon as the final whistle blows, they wouldn't dream of looking at a Lawbook.

Ed: Well, let's be fair. I never read the laws when I was a player, and I doubt if I'd have been much better off if I'd tried! The Lawbook is a lot more user-friendly now, but parts of the game are complicated, for sure. That's why I think the communication revolution is so important. I can remember, on my way up, refereeing one of the top clubs in England, and afterwards the captain said, 'Thank God someone's willing to talk to us!' So as late as the mid-Eighties, many senior referees weren't exactly looking for things to say to players.

Derek: And that was understandable. For years and years, the party line had been: *The less said, the better.* Back in 1970 there was a conference of referee societies in England, and they were told that only three signals were needed – scrum, penalty and try – and they had to be unobtrusive. They were definitely *not* for the spectators' benefit.

Ed: It was a very conservative game in those days.

Derek: Your refereeing wouldn't have made many friends in high places then.

Ed: Probably not. When I first started refereeing, I used to be criticised for talking too much, especially for going into a long account of why I'd given the penalty. I remember someone very experienced in the game saying to me, 'You carry on, young man – because if you go up the ladder, you won't have *time* to give out all that nonsense.' And he was right. The game's so fast nowadays. The three quicks – quick penalty, quick free kick, quick throw-in – have added a whole new dimension to rugby. By the time I've blown the whistle and said, 'Blue No. 5, over the top', they've tapped the ball and gone!

Derek: You don't even say 'penalty kick'.

Ed: I don't need to. The whistle says it for me. Long blast, they know it's serious, my arm goes up, they know who's got the penalty. It's instantaneous.

'DON'T TAKE IT!'

Derek: Now here's the dilemma. You're very quick and clear and positive, which the players like, because it lets them tap and run. But the offence may be serious. You may want to speak to the guilty party.

Ed: In that case I'll say: *'Don't take it.'* I've got to weigh up the situation fast, decide that I can't let this offence pass, and stop the game. Some teams get quite aggrieved about it.

Derek: Understandably.

Ed: If the captain comes over, I'll say, 'Sorry, skipper, but this has got to be sorted out now.' In the Neath–Fiji game, when I penalised the Fiji guy twice in two minutes for coming over the top, Gareth Llewellyn couldn't believe his ears when I said, 'Stop – don't take it!' Neath were only a few yards from the goal line. I told the Fiji player, 'You kill one more ball and you're *gone.'* And I told Gareth, 'That guy's been cautioned.'

Derek: Why tell him?

Ed: Because I knew what those Welsh boys would have done, otherwise.

Derek: They would have taken steps to discourage the Fiji player from repeating the offence?

Ed: Taken steps? Yes. Bloody big steps, too. And when I talked to him, I made it clear that I was talking to everybody. Neath knew I would apply the same standard to them, if necessary.

Derek: It occurs to me that by the time the referee's said, 'Don't take it,' they might well have taken it.

Ed: If that happens, don't stop it. Don't bring them back. Just live with it, and catch up with the offender at some other time. But it's best to seize the moment if you can. Something in you just clicks and you know: *this is the time.* Everything's moving so rapidly that you have to create a chance to communicate *now,* because that communication is essential to your control.

Derek: Okay. That's an example where you wanted to get your point across to them. If – as you said – players like to be talked to, apart from hearing why they'd been penalised, what is it they want to hear from you?

Ed: Well, it's hard to cover everything in one sentence, but preventative refereeing is one thing they appreciate – talking so that I don't need to blow – and another thing they like is what someone called my 'Go-go' refereeing, because I'm always shouting 'Go on, go on!'

Derek: To confirm that the ball's still in play? You're not about to blow up?

Ed: Exactly. But the reality is that I'm talking from the first minute to the last.

Derek: I've made a transcript of every word you said during the Pilkington Cup Final in 1994, Bath versus Leicester. Very interesting.

Ed: Very long! I worked hard that day, but . . . The game refused to flow. I felt sorry for the spectators, at times.

Derek: On the other hand, difficult games probably reach parts of you that other games don't, which is why I found your comments useful. I identified a dozen different elements in what you said, and the way you said it, that I think any referee should be aware of. The first is speed. There's very little time for the referee to get his message across, because everything happens so fast, but you packed a lot of very brief messages into a very short space of time. For instance, when the second scrum formed, here's what you said to the front rows:

Now we go in when I say. Wait, Graham. WAIT! Darren, get your hand down and keep it down. Come on, scrum-half. (A few seconds pause) *Free kick!*

All that began, and happened, and was over in no time at all. I mean, a junior referee would still be clearing his throat.

Ed: That's the speed of the senior game. The scrums were a headache throughout that game. If you look at my words, I had time to say three things. First – don't engage too soon. Second – props bind legally. Third – put the ball in. Unfortunately the front rows were too interested in fighting their little civil war, the ball didn't go in, and I penalised Bath for delay. In the first fifteen minutes I gave four free kicks for delay at the put-in. Both teams got penalised. So words alone weren't enough!

Derek: If they won't listen, you've got to make them listen.

Ed: After that we got the ball in more quickly.

Derek: But the front rows were always far too eager to get to grips with each other. Here's a typical moment as you kept them apart:

Wait! Wait! Wait! WAIT! WAIT! WAIT! Thank you, Richard.

Three things impressed me there: repetition, loudness, and then sudden contrast. Whereas I might have said 'Wait!' two or three times, you said it six times, without pause – and far louder than I would, considering you're only a foot away from the scrum. In the end you were bawling at them, full-strength. Then, as they engaged, your voice instantly changed, and your *Thank you, Richard* to the scrum-half was quiet and relaxed.

Ed: Well, he wasn't the problem, was he? It was the six guys glaring at each other who were the problem, and I kept shouting to hammer the message into their skulls. Once they engaged properly – problem over.

Derek: Sure. But many a referee can't change gears as slickly as that. The front row gives the referee a hell of a hard time, and then he snaps at the scrum-half: 'Come on! Hurry up! Get the ball in! No delay!'

Ed: That's no good. The poor scrum-half's done nothing wrong, so don't make him feel victimised. You need him as a friend, if possible. Tone of voice does matter. You've got to be able to bollock this guy one second and encourage that guy the next.

CUT IT SHORT

Derek: Probably the most important lesson I learned from listening to you referee that game was brevity.

Ed: Absolutely essential. The game's played at such a pace that you haven't got time or breath for speeches, and they can't take them in, anyway.

Derek: In fact, you very rarely used more than two words to get across a message.

Ed: Suits me nicely. I can remember two words.

Derek: Here are some that struck me most. Scrum collapses, or a tackle ends in a pile-up, you shout: 'Come up! Come up! Come away! Come away!'

Ed: I like a positive message. You hear referees say things like 'That's enough,' or 'Be careful,' when there's a great heap of tangled bodies. The player has to work out what *That's enough* means.

Derek: He has to go through a little mental exercise, at a time when his brain isn't at its best.

Ed: Whereas 'Come up!' is a simple, positive order. Sometimes it's just 'Up! Up!' He doesn't have to interpret that, just *do* it. If there's fists flying and I can stop the fight, I'll say 'Go away! Go away!' to separate the sides. They know what it means, they don't need to work it out. Something like 'Cut it out!' or 'Beat it!' is less immediate. Less effective, I find.

Derek: When the ball goes from line-out to stand-off and he kicks ahead, you shout 'Stay, forwards!' or sometimes just 'Still!'

Ed: To keep them onside, yes. And sometimes I'll shout 'You're OK!' when the winger, or whoever, has put them all onside.

Derek: At rucks and mauls you often say 'Rear feet, rear feet!' – again, to keep players onside who are standing off the ruck or maul. At penalty kicks you sometimes say 'Go away! Go away!', just to get the penalised team moving back. At line-outs you'll say 'Ten, Leicester!' or 'Ten, Bath!' to get their backs the full ten metres behind. Even when you blow up for an offence, the explanation's very brief – 'Knocked forward' or 'Number 2 offside' or 'Hands on the floor' (for handling in the ruck) or 'Pulling back' (for jersey tugging) or 'Straight over' (for going over the top of a ruck or maul) or 'Compressing' (the line-out) or 'Straight through' (player going through the line-out) or 'Pulling down' (collapsing a maul). At penalties or free kicks, you say 'Looking ten' to get the penalised team back ten metres. And best of all, when there's no offence and no reason to stop, you shout 'Go on, go on, go on!' You do a lot of urging.

Ed: If I feel they might have thought the ball got knocked on, I'll shout 'Went back!' and then 'Go on!', just so that they know I saw it. You're right, I do urge them to *go on! go on!* when there's no reason to stop. After all, I enjoy seeing running rugby, and since there was precious little of it that afternoon, I encouraged every bit I saw.

Derek: Half an hour into the match, Leicester won possession at a maul in midfield, and they held the ball at the rear, and you were shouting, 'Let's do something! Let's do it!'

Ed: And they didn't, did they? I knew I was going to have to blow up soon, because that maul wasn't moving an inch. But Leicester didn't use the ball, it disappeared back into the maul, I blew for a scrum. It was that sort of a match.

Derek: A bit later, at a ruck, you were actually telling players where the ball was and how to get it. You said, 'There it is! There it is! Underneath. Lift him.'

Ed: If one team has got the ball won at a ruck, they should be able to use it. The alternative is that everything grinds to a halt again. If I can speed up delivery, I'll do it.

Derek: Is that why you shout 'Let go! Let go!' at rucks?

Ed: Yes. If the opposition hasn't got a hope of winning the ball, I don't want them interfering with it. Let it go, let's see it out and moving.

Derek: Something I paid special attention to was the way that you used the occasional breaks in play to get a message across. For instance, when a drop at goal went wide, you found time to tell the scrum-half: 'Got to get it in quick, Rich. They're going to fool about all day if we let them. Get it in.' Then, while the kicker was preparing a penalty kick at goal, you warned the captain about his prop: 'Deano – have a word with Darren on the scrummage. I want him up a bit more on this side, all right?' As the players ran to a line-out, you gave one guy a quiet word of advice: 'Don't get involved in the personal stuff! Someone's going to go walkies in a minute . . .' When the full back made a mark, you used the few seconds' break to say, 'Jon – keep the mauls on their feet.' And so on.

Ed: That's the only way the referee can manage the modern game. There are so few chances to make your point, you've got to seize every one of them. And make every word count, because there's no time for speeches.

Derek: Except when there was a brawl early in the game and you stopped play and called the captains together.

Ed: Even then, it's a very short speech. They know what's coming. I don't need to spell it out.

Derek: In fact, your first speech to them was exactly eleven words long. You said:

Cut this shit out. It's pointless, it's stupid. Get a grip.

Ed: That was enough. I'd already awarded a penalty, so the captains had a good opportunity to talk to their players. That was what I wanted – the captains to be responsible.

WORDS AS LEVERS

Derek: There was another scrap, much later. More of a wrestling match, really, and miles away from the ball. Here's what you said to the captains then:

Tell you what, boys, every one of us here is letting ourselves down. [Dean Richards said that he hadn't hit anyone.] No, nor me. I haven't punched anybody. Nor Jon [Hall, the Bath captain]. Get to grips, OK? Get to grips. Quick one.

Ed: Meaning, have a quick word with your team. I felt we were making ourselves look foolish on what should have been a great rugby occasion. I tried to use that idea as leverage on the players, because I genuinely felt that their performance hadn't been worthy of them. All that afternoon I was trying to work *with* the players, to find a way to jack up their game.

Derek: Bath had Victor Ubogu, the England prop. Very powerful man with a very short fuse. He called on all your powers of diplomacy, I thought.

Ed: Victor made a tackle, both teams piled into the ruck, and Victor's back got badly twisted. Bath handled the ball in the ruck. I blew for the penalty.

Derek: And here's what you said, immediately after the whistle:

Let go of him! Let go. Let go. Watch his back! Watch his back, watch his back! That's a hand in, Bath.

Ed: Which was when Victor got up and threw a punch, and missed. But it was a big punch. So I blew for that.

Derek: And here's what you said then:

Go back ten! [The teams separated.] Come here, Vic, come here. [Ubogu was reluctant to do so.] No, come here. Jon! Go away, Andy. Go away, Neil, go away. Jon! [The captain joins them.] Come over here, boys. Vic, I didn't see the beginning of it. I saw the last bit when your back was turned over, I know it wasn't very nice. The original offence, Jon, you were playing the ball on the floor, denying them possession. That's what the original penalty was for. Vic – blame me, OK? Blame me.

And Ubogu walked away, looking slightly less angry. What interests me is you never mentioned his punch.

Ed: What was there to say? There was nothing to say. Basically, what I was trying to do was buy time, and get Victor off the ceiling. And I didn't want him to go away feeling that I'd penalised *him*. I was looking for a way to calm him down. Avoid future trouble.

Derek: You're quite willing to apologise to players, aren't you? I mean, here's a selection of remarks:

Okay, I didn't see it. Sorry. Apologise. Come back.

and at a scrum:

If there's a problem, it's my fault.

and, from a line-out:

I didn't see that . . . Sorry, Deano, I was watching something else . . .

and at another scrum, when one front row wasn't ready to engage:

Sorry, boys, I was at fault.

Now, I know a few referees who feel that *any* apology damages their authority.

Ed: I think it strengthens mine. This goes back to the question of honesty. If you've got it wrong, and they know it, then say so. It shouldn't weaken your control. You can apologise one minute and hammer someone the next. Why not?

Derek: I noticed there's room for humour, too. After Tony Swift, the Bath winger, chased a very long diagonal kick, and scored, you said to him: 'Was that planned?'

Ed: Purely spontaneous remark. I'm not a comedian, but it does no harm to behave like a human being occasionally. In that game, it helped greatly that I knew all the players and I could use their names – Deano, Andy, Graham, Rich, Nige and so on.

Derek: Communication works both ways. How much are you prepared to take from a player?

Ed: As long as he's not questioning my authority, I'll talk to anybody. I prefer the remarks to be channelled through one person, and preferably the captain, but if there's a break in play and one scrum-half says, 'Can you watch their scrum-half – he's pulling my shirt as I put the ball in,' I'll say, 'Thanks, I will look.'

Derek: Scrum-halves have become increasingly chatty. At rucks or mauls they're constantly telling the referee, 'I can see the ball – there it is, it's coming, it's coming.' Does that make your job easier?

Ed: No. I understand why they do it, but if I have to rely on players telling me where the ball is, then I've got a problem. The scrum-half may be guessing. He may be hoping. At ruck and maul, the most important thing for the referee is identifying the ball, and then moving away. Once I've done that, I'm happy. If I can't identify the ball, I blow the whistle. If I rely on the scrum-half telling me, then he's running the game, not me.

Derek: He would claim that he's trying to help you.

THE EPIDEMIC OF APPEALS

Ed: Of course he would. Players are always coming up to the referee and wanting to be helpful. The fact remains that they are not completely unbiased. Now, the amount of talk that a referee will accept is down to him. My advice is to be very guarded. Be ready to pull up the drawbridge if you feel the players are pushing their luck. Personally, I quite like a bit of banter with players, I quite like players to talk to me. Not *at* me, but *to* me. What I won't take is an endless stream of complaints. I'll tell them to shut up.

Derek: I remember hearing you say, 'The more you talk, the less notice I'll take.'

Ed: Yes, because I know they're just trying to talk me into giving a penalty. One thing I detest as a referee is players who appeal for things. I detest it because, if I make my decision their way, it looks as if I'm *responding* to the appeal.

Derek: And then the opposition start to think, *Hey, if we appeal, maybe we'll get a decision our way . . .*

Ed: Exactly. It's infectious.

Derek: And it's spreading. Even at international level, players like Rory Underwood dive on – or near – the ball in the in-goal, and then instantly look around and appeal for a try.

Ed: They're putting pressure on the referee.

Derek: And it can happen to junior referees, can't it? In one of the first matches I refereed, the stand-off dropped for goal, missed by a yard – and all fifteen of his team leaped in the air!

Ed: Like I said, it's a disease. Often I've said to players, 'I'm not going to give it if you appeal. No matter how obvious it is, if you appeal, I'll ignore it.'

Derek: At one point in that Pilkington Cup Final, you told a player, 'I ain't gonna give it. You know me better than that.' It must make a difference if they know you're on the international panel.

Ed: I suppose it's like anything else: refereeing's a lot easier when you're established than when you're trying to *become* established.

Derek: A very successful American once said to me, 'The trick of becoming a multi-millionaire is to make your second million first.'

Ed: Absolutely right! Get to the top, and start there!

The Unreliable Lawbook

Derek: Suppose I want to be a referee. Is it really all that important for me to read the Lawbook until I know it inside-out?

Ed: Absolutely essential.

Derek: Why?

Ed: Because you've got to know the letter of the law. That's the essential framework of the game. You've got to be able to fall back on it.

Derek: But in many important areas of the game, if I fall back on the Lawbook I'll do myself a nasty injury, because what the Lawbook tells me to do is not the way the game is refereed. In fact, there are several areas of the game that are refereed in direct opposition to what the Lawbook says! And refereed by top referees, too.

Ed: I see you've got a list.

Derek: I do. Six examples. Mostly about winning possession.

Ed: Let's hear them.

SIX FIXES

Derek: I call them Fixes, because I reckon they've been brought in to fix something that wasn't working. The first Fix is you let the scrum-half burrow in a ruck, and the second is you let the team winning the ball hand-ruck it out. In both cases the law prohibits hands in the ruck. The third Fix is you give favoured treatment at a scrum to the scrum-half of the team that's won the ball. You let him pick up the ball when, in exactly the same circumstances, you don't let the opposing scrum-half touch it. That's contrary to law. Next, you let a tackled player roll over, reach out and plonk the ball down and then hold it in place. The law says he must release it or play it immediately. How many Fixes is that?

Ed: Four.

Derek: Fifth, at a tackle you let players arriving on the scene step over the ball and then go one pace forward and make contact with the opposition. No justification in law for that. And finally, the advantage law says clearly that 'a mere opportunity to gain advantage is not enough' but you say that an opportunity to take advantage *is* enough, provided that the team has speedy possession and enough space to use it. Those are the six Fixes. Now, suppose I was a new, unqualified referee taking my exam to get my badge. Suppose the examiner described those six situations, and I said they were all quite legal . . .

Ed: You'd fail.

Derek: So I tell him what I've been coached, which is that they're all contrary to law, and I get my badge, and I go out and find I have to referee completely differently.

Ed: That's the reality. Not for a minute would I blame the coaches or examiners. They've got to work with the Lawbook as it exists.

Derek: Sure. I blame the Lawbook. It's wrong. And I blame the International Rugby Board, simply because the IRB is supposed to be the guardian of the game, and it's failing in its duty. And while I'm at it, I might as well blame the various senior Unions for allowing all this to happen, since they really run the IRB.

Ed: You don't blame me, then.

Derek: Stick around. There's more to come.

Ed: I think you're a bit hard on the IRB. All these Fixes, as you call them, came out of international conferences that were organised under the general umbrella of the IRB. I mean, the whole idea was to improve the game, and a lot of very experienced people – coaches, players, referees, administrators – did a lot of hard work. It seems a bit unfair to blame them for their efforts.

Derek: It's not their efforts I blame. I *like* their efforts. What I don't like is this veil of secrecy around their decisions.

Ed: Nothing's secret. Everything was openly agreed.

Derek: Well, it never reached me, and I'm a typical grassroots referee. I get my new Lawbook every season. If these Fixes aren't in it, how am I supposed to know they exist?

Ed: There's no easy answer, apart from the fact that the game is immensely complex. That's one of the beauties of it, in my opinion. It *is* complex, and when you compare refereeing a game with reading a Lawbook . . . sometimes the two don't marry, and I think that's the point you're making.

Derek: No, it's not.

Ed: Well, you lost me, then.

Derek: My point is that the two don't marry because these international conferences which you've attended have deliberately moved the game away from the Lawbook. The IRB has quietly approved all these Fixes that came out of the conferences, but it hasn't put them in the laws – God alone knows why. Complexity has bugger-all to do with it. Pardon my Anglo-Saxon. I get steamed-up about this.

Ed: What I think you've got to bear in mind is there were some really difficult areas in the game that were causing serious problems for everyone – players and referees.

Derek: Such as?

Ed: Let's take the example of the use of the hand in the ruck. For a number of years, if the ball was at the rear of a ruck, and the opposition had absolutely no opportunity to get possession, and a player of the team winning the ball flipped it back with his hand – I never penalised that.

Derek: Known as hand-rucking.

Ed: Yes.

Derek: And this is very different from handling the ball in the middle of the ruck, before one team or the other has won possession.

Ed: Right. We're talking about a situation where the ruck is very nearly over and the ball just needs a final nudge to get it out. At one of our RFU conferences, some coaches said they were mystified by referees' inconsistency – some referees penalised hand-rucking, some didn't. It was thoroughly discussed and agreed that when the ball was obviously won by one team, hand-rucking was acceptable because it was a practical way of getting the ball back into play quicker.

Derek: Everyone wanted it?

Ed: Yes. Hand-rucking's advantageous to the players at the ruck, and to the game in general because the ball's in play faster, and to the referee because – as we've often said – it's much easier to referee when you can identify the ball.

Derek: And they all find hand-rucking easy to understand?

Ed: No problem that I know of. It's a very practical solution.

Derek: And have other countries had the same idea?

Ed: Yes. It's applied all over the world.

Derek: So why isn't it in the Lawbook? And don't tell me this particular Fix is just an interpretation of the existing ruck law. It's obviously a change to law, just like all the other Fixes. But the Lawbook isn't changed. This is what baffles me.

THE OLD COMMUNICATION PROBLEM

Ed: I sometimes think the lawmakers are reluctant to commit themselves to a form of words. Drafting law can be very difficult.

Derek: If you're right, that's a pretty limp excuse. If the lawmakers can't make law they shouldn't have the job. Anyway, this hand-rucking Fix has been put into words already, hasn't it?

Ed: Certainly. The conference decisions went into a report and that report was circulated to Referee Societies. One of the decisions was to allow hand-rucking as an experimental interpretation. So the information was supposed to reach all referees via their Societies. But, as you and I know, probably not more than a third of members actually attend their Society meetings. And very few of those attend all meetings . . .

Derek: So the hard fact is that two-thirds of all referees never get to hear about these Fixes. They carry on refereeing according to the Lawbook.

Ed: The good news – in England, at least – is that the RFU is setting up a data base for all 4,000 referees who are members of Referees' Societies. In future, they will get all refereeing information sent directly to their homes.

Derek: Well, that's a start, I suppose.

Ed: And there's always rugby on television, of course. That's a great medium for spreading information.

Derek: So I'm told. It can also be demoralising to the young referee, when he penalises something and then goes home and sees a top referee allow the same thing in an international match. Poor bloke doesn't know where he stands. Especially as the players watch television too.

Ed: It can be a problem.

Derek: It's happened to me, many a time. Players say: 'They get away with it at Twickenham. Why can't we do it?'

Ed: The point I'm trying to make is that all these Fixes – which have actually been approved by the various IRB conferences – are meant to be *positive.* I mean, these conferences weren't just a jolly. People didn't fly thousands of miles just to have a few beers together. The aim was to improve the game internationally, especially the consistency of the refereeing. Everyone was trying to find practical solutions to difficult areas of the game. Abolishing the Fixes and refereeing strictly by the book won't improve the game. Quite the reverse.

Derek: I don't want them abolished! I like them! If the IRB has approved them, why doesn't it simply spread the word? Why does it have to make life so difficult for the poor bloody ref who's out in the sticks with just two things to help him: his whistle and his Lawbook, one of which turns out to be incomplete and unreliable? If these Fixes matter so much, shouldn't every referee know about them?

Ed: Even if you sent everyone the information, you can't assume they'd all read it. 90% of referees just want an 80-minute trot-about on a Saturday afternoon.

Derek: And if I didn't know you better, I'd say that was patronising. Are you telling me that all referees don't deserve an equal chance to referee as well as they can?

Ed: I'm saying that skill levels have a *bearing* on whether or not you can apply these Fixes. Hand-rucking's no good if a team can't begin to ruck the ball, and so on.

Derek: I don't agree. The skill levels may affect how *often* you can apply the Fixes, but nearly all of them would help the game at *any* level. Hand rucking? Scrum-half burrowing? Privileged possession at the scrum? Letting the tackled player roll over and place? Nothing terribly difficult there. Even your local 3rd XV could benefit from being allowed to play like that.

Ed: But a lot of what we've been talking about will come naturally to any referee who's played a bit of rugby himself, and who understands what the game's about. If he's got a real understanding, a real feel for the game, he doesn't need a big book.

Derek: But he'll need a small book. Even you need a Lawbook.

Ed: Yes. He's definitely going to need some guidelines. Some help.

Derek: And what I'm saying is: Let's give them to him! Look: suppose the proverbial man from Mars arrived and saw this situation. He'd say, 'Hullo, the IRB has a Laws Committee and every year they make a few law changes, they hold a Press Conference to publicise them, they circulate the changes to all Unions, they change the Lawbook. But – hullo, hullo, what have we here? Every year the IRB sponsors an international conference, and *they* make several *different* law changes which *never* go into the Lawbook! They're supposed to improve the game but only the privileged few get to know! Is this any way to run a railroad?'

Ed: You've got to bear in mind that the IRB Conferences can't rewrite the laws. They have no authority to change the official Lawbook. Only the IRB itself can do that.

NO SECRETS, PLEASE

Derek: Sure. But the decisions of the Conferences change the way referees *apply* the laws. So even if they can't alter the words on the page, the Conferences can change their meaning. The Conferences may not have authority but they've certainly got power.

Ed: Maybe referees have too much power! Some people in the game are worried about that. They think the referee's control plays too big a part in deciding the outcome. Not that he's unfair. The problem is the sheer complexity of some areas of play. So the IRB has set up a sort of task force to review the laws. Those involved are all very experienced men, with wide knowledge of the game. Six major Unions are taking part. For example, the RFU is using its County Championship to experiment with a couple of changes. One is allowing players to pull down the maul; another is always allowing players on their feet to handle the ball on the ground at the breakdown.

Derek: Strictly limited to the County Championship?

Ed: At present, yes. Just an experiment.

Derek: If it works, will we all hear about it?

Ed: I certainly hope so.

Derek: Me too. I'm fed up with top referees being let in on the secret, while the rest of us are treated like second-class citizens.

Ed: Communications could definitely be better.

Derek: It's not such a huge problem, after all. Listen to this: I've just scribbled down what could be added to the ruck law to cover hand-rucking:

When a team has clearly won the ball at a ruck, any of the hindmost players in the ruck may knock the ball back from the rear of the ruck with his hand.

Derek: What do you think?

Ed: Looks good to me. Certainly the IRB have an open mind. They'll be analysing the outcome of all experiments very closely.

Derek: It's simple. All these Fixes are simple. You could write them on half a sheet of paper and still have room for a map of the London Underground.

Outlook

Derek: How do you see the future of the game? Some people say we need two Lawbooks – one for professional rugby, one for amateur.

Ed: We've already got two games. There's no question about that.

Derek: What's the difference? Can you sum it up, briefly?

Ed: Yes. Speed.

Derek: I see. Not skill, or tactics?

Ed: Well, speed *involves* skill and tactics. It's the sheer pace at which everything is carried out.

Derek: But at the top level, is it still carried out within the same set of laws?

Ed: Yes and no. Let me give you two examples. The last time I was in Paris, I refereed France against Ireland. A few weeks later I refereed Yatton 3rds against Clevedon 3rds.

Derek: Real grassroots rugby, there.

Ed: And my philosophy at both matches was exactly the same. I tried to do the same things – manage the scrums, prevent penalties if possible, get the ball away and moving, play advantage, keep people on their feet, and so on. The difference was, at Yatton I always had time to do what I wanted. In Paris, there were moments when I wanted to blow the whistle, but it was too late! In the fraction of a second it took me to think, the ball was miles away! Everything was done at 100 miles an hour.

Derek: And France won, 45-10.

Ed: Speed is the difference. At the senior level, the players are driving forward the law changes, through the pace at which they're playing the game. And I think that will continue for a number of years.

Derek: D'you think we'll need two Lawbooks?

Ed: I hope not. One thing I like about the existing Lawbook is its flexibility. Many of the laws tell me what I can't allow – but they don't tell me what I *can* allow. So they just leave a door open for the referee who's got a good feel for the game, who appreciates the great variety of play on offer. As far as rugby is concerned, it's not a black-and-white world with no in-between. A referee who realises that can adjust his refereeing to the needs of the game, and still be true to the laws.

Derek: You've said before that skill levels are improving, and it's obvious that players are fitter and faster and stronger. So can we all look forward to improved laws and a golden age of rugby?

Ed: Well, that depends on the players' attitude. Whatever law changes anyone wants to make, I believe that if the players want to be positive and play rugby, the laws are already there for them to do so. The other side of that coin is this: you can change whatever laws you like, but you will still get good games, and you will still get bad games.

Derek: That is not what sponsors and television want to hear.

Ed: No, but it's the hard truth. When the game suddenly went open, there were clubs and players – and some Unions too – who thought the future was going to be one big pot of gold, and they've had a nasty shock. Rugby is not soccer. It has a different appeal. Does an audience exist for wall-to-wall rugby? People can easily get fed up with it.

Derek: A match with a lot of penalty goals and one lucky try is not what they pay to see.

Ed: You're right. In my opinion, we're far too quick to blame the laws, blame the referee, blame the coaching, blame the weather. The one thing we don't blame is our *attitude*. It's our attitude that's not right.

Derek: Is this a cultural thing?

Ed: Partly.

CLASH OF CULTURES

Derek: When England beat Western Samoa in 1995, and for the last quarter England just slowed everything down and played out time, I remember thinking: the All Blacks wouldn't have done that.

Ed: They certainly wouldn't. In the '95 World Cup, I ran the touch when New Zealand beat Japan 145-17. First time in my life I'd been involved in a game like that. I'm convinced that at half-time, any British side would have relaxed. It's in our culture: we like to beat a team, but we don't like to beat them down. The All Blacks never relaxed. There were only four scrums and five line-outs in the whole match. They just went and went and went, flat out, right to the final whistle.

Derek: Would Australia do the same, given the chance?

Ed: Certainly. If they were beating England, they'd certainly keep going! They really like to win. I watched Australia put 70-odd points on Western Samoa in 1994. Samoa had a lot of good players, but Australia were simply awesome that evening. And again, they just didn't stop.

Derek: What do you think creates these cultural differences? I know the climate in Australia helps, but it rains and it blows in New Zealand. They have mud, just like us.

Ed: It comes back to attitude. All through the Southern Hemisphere they go on the field with one thought in mind: they want to run the ball. I don't say they never kick – you see plenty of aerial ping-pong in South Africa, especially on the high veldt – and I don't say you never see a forward slog. They don't chuck it about like basketball. But their priority is 15-man rugby. In some of our international matches the winger never touches the ball. They wouldn't tolerate that Down Under.

Derek: Nor would the crowd.

Ed: And everyone knows it. Australia is very professional about getting bums on seats. They're years ahead of us. When I was there in 1993, players in Australia told me that they were entertainers. That's something the professional players and the clubs in Britain still haven't grasped. The Australians were very clear about it: they got paid to play rugby, the spectators paid good money to be entertained, and if they weren't entertained, the turnstiles wouldn't click next time!

Derek: So winning is not enough?

Ed: Not nearly enough. From what I've seen, players in Australia and New Zealand and South Africa aren't any more skilful than our players in the Northern Hemisphere, but their attitude's better. They know that if they don't take a positive attitude, they're going to be playing in ghost towns.

Derek: If they don't perform, they won't get paid.

Ed: Simple as that.

Derek: What has this done to their refereeing?

Ed: Because their game has been switched on to this entertainment mode for a few years, they've had time to focus on the things that really matter to them. For instance, the Australians don't take the scrum as seriously as we do. Their attitude is very straightforward: *you've* offended – so *we* should win the ball. If we put it in a bit squint, who cares? Provided the ball's not thrown in front of the No. 8's feet, they're all fairly relaxed about it.

Derek: That approach would upset a few hookers I know.

Ed: Brian Moore argued strongly that crooked feeds were de-skilling the hooker's role. He said you don't allow crooked throw-ins; why allow crooked put-ins? But the reality is that a lot of international teams now play a prop as hooker, and invariably he doesn't even strike for the ball against the head.

Derek: Interesting. What else gets bent in the Southern Hemisphere, besides the put-in?

Ed: Very often, if a scrum collapses, play carries on – sometimes for quite a long time.

Derek: Now, the law couldn't be clearer about that. Scrum collapses, referee must blow immediately.

Ed: And that's for safety's sake. But in Australia and New Zealand, provided the ball's coming back, they carry on. What matters to them is getting the ball away and moving it around the field.

Derek: And I expect they like a bit of advantage.

Ed: They play advantage to the absolute limit.

Derek: You've refereed all these countries, so you must have noticed one little trick of theirs. When the opposition puts in a big kick, and the full back or winger is about to catch it, he's often got two or three large teammates hanging about, just in front of him.

Ed: It's no accident, is it? It's obstruction, and it's a nightmare for the referee.

Derek: Those team-mates can put on quite an act. They can make it look as if they're jumping for the ball. Or they can dodge about and seem to be busy, but the fact is they're a couple of yards from where the ball's going to land. They're making a barrier, aren't they?

Ed: Of course. It's something that's been copied from Rugby League, where players are very skilled at blocking the path of the man chasing the kick. We can learn a lot from Rugby League's lines of running, but not obstruction.

Derek: Mind you, the same sort of thing's been known to happen in Europe.

Ed: Sure. They're just craftier in the Southern Hemisphere.

Derek: But they do entertain. I mean, they score plenty of points, and a lot come from tries. You very rarely hear of a low-scoring game Down Under.

Ed: I'm over-simplifying, but my impression is that we in Britain play rugby like chess – we move a square at a time. Our culture's conservative and we sometimes play conservatively. They don't. When I refereed club games in Australia and South Africa, I realised their first impulse was to pass the ball. They play a high-risk game. Their players demand a positive, creative approach. If you're in a rugby match and you never touch the ball, you go surfing instead.

Derek: Well, that's a refreshing approach.

Ed: It can be. It can also be too loose. Play becomes sloppy. A high-risk game needs high skills. I've taken matches where players were rushing around like headless chickens! Even in the Super Twelves, an awful lot of tries got scored through bad tackling. It's easy for an attack to look good if the defence is full of holes, isn't it? But there's no denying that everyone gets involved, even if they have to skip a page of the Lawbook here and there to do it.

Derek: Is there much contact between players and referees in the Southern Hemisphere?

Ed: Not that I'm aware of. Quite the opposite, in fact. Traditionally, in South Africa the referees have always been isolated from the players. I refereed a match in the '95 World Cup, and afterwards the chap looking after me suggested that we went to the referees' room. I said, 'Where will the players be?' He said that they'd be at the post-match function. I said, 'Well, that's where I'm going.' He found that very strange.

Derek: What's this referees' room?

Ed: It's a clubhouse for referees. All the referees gather there. Everybody in there is a referee.

Derek: Good God. That's as bad as a conference of psychiatrists.

Ed: What they haven't done in South Africa is mix with the players after the game, which is when you've got to show your face. So they've become isolated.

Derek: What's your experience of Southern Hemisphere teams coming to Britain? What do they think of our referees?

Ed: National squads have all done their homework, so they know what to expect. Club sides are often pretty apprehensive, full of questions about what our referees will be hot on, to the point that some are almost filled with trepidation! They expect us to be very strict.

Derek: Perhaps what that means is that we play and referee according to the official IRB Lawbook, whereas some countries have their own funny ways.

Ed: Well, let's examine that. For fifty years, the IRB has been granting Dispensations to some Unions to experiment with law changes. Take the Australian Dispensation – no gain in ground for kicks direct to touch, except penalties, from outside the 25, as it then was. The Aussies played like that for decades, until everyone accepted it. The 'cricket-catch' at a knock-on was another experiment that became law, in 1973. Before that, any fumble was an infringement! The yard-wide gap in the line-out was an experiment first. So was blood replacement, and the Sin Bin, and upping the try from 3 points to 4, then 5. On we go. The French are testing an interesting idea now: if a team must go to uncontested scrums, they lose a player! Front rows are suddenly stronger, I'm told!

Derek: So the moral is: don't knock it if you haven't tried it.

OPEN-MINDED

Ed: Oh, we can definitely learn. I was refereeing in the United States once, and when a guy scored a try, he let out a great big howl. One of those cowboy whoops. I mean, he put on quite a performance. I quietly said to him, 'There's no need for that.' He said, 'Why not?' So I said, 'Well, we don't do that.' And he said, 'Well, we do, over here. That's how we celebrate!' Straightaway it came home to me: *You're not in England now.* All too often we assume that everything we do is how the rest of the world should do it. The truth is we've got a lot to learn from other cultures. For years now, I've been telling anyone at Twickenham who'll listen that we've got to get more international experience by travelling beyond Europe.

Derek: You travel a lot. What have you learned? Surprise me.

Ed: Well . . . I got invited to referee at the Uruguay Sevens Tournament.

Derek: Uruguay . . . that's a hell of a long way to go.

Ed: 26 hours on the plane. Sat next to a woman whose baby cried all the way. Didn't get any sleep.

Derek: And Uruguay's not exactly famous for its rugby.

Ed: Brilliant tournament. Top teams from most of the major rugby-playing nations. Superb organisation. I had a wonderful time. New Zealand beat France in the Final, 31-25. After extra time, again!

Derek: And what can we learn from South American rugby?

Ed: Some of their ball-playing skills were a revelation. I've never seen players dribble a rugby ball with such speed and skill! They went through the defence like Ryan Giggs.

Derek: Did they like your refereeing?

Ed: They liked the way I played advantage to the hilt. They were very surprised when I didn't keep knocking a team back ten, when I stopped play to warn the player or the players for not retiring. And they got very frustrated when I enforced the tackle law concerning the arriving player.

Derek: After a tackle, next man to play the ball must be on his feet?

Ed: Yes. Often their player would be on one knee as he flipped the ball back. They couldn't see any point in penalising him. They'd say: 'But we were winning the ball anyway. Maybe his knee touched the ground, but that didn't affect the opposition's chances. And we got the ball back in play. What's wrong with that? They were a bit baffled.

Derek: So what's your answer? What is wrong with it?

Ed: What's wrong with a pass that's only a bit forward? You can't referee like that. Either it's forward or it's not. Same with arriving players not on their feet at the tackle. They've become the curse of the game. They turn the tackle zone into a pile-up, with horizontal bodies stacked like logs, and the ball totally trapped. That's why the IRB wants the game to be played by players on their feet. South American rugby doesn't always agree. They say, let's win the ball! Let's get on!

Derek: They like their rugby to sparkle.

Ed: They do.

Derek: I take it you believe in national characteristics.

Ed: Certainly. I've found that refereeing Latin-American teams is no great problem when they're reasonably happy and self-confident, but when they're down, they go a long way down. If they get upset with themselves, and upset with the referee – watch out. Communication suddenly becomes very difficult indeed.

Derek: Are the French and the Italians the same?

Ed: Yes. Some things don't seem compatible with their culture. Certainly, at international level they find it very hard to come to terms with 'Back ten, back ten'. Start doing that to them, without solving the problem, and you'll be marching them back all afternoon. On the plus side, they're quite happy to play advantage to the extreme.

Derek: But French club rugby is no place for the faint-hearted, is it?

Ed: It can be a very hard, very physical game, especially in the line-out. French teams can get frustrated very quickly if the line-out's going badly for them, and they might lose control and do something silly. I've always found that the best approach to the French is to show a degree of sympathy and get them on your side. The moment they think the referee's *against* them, he's got bigger problems than they have! So you've got to cajole them a bit more, and take into account the cultural differences. They can be difficult but they can be brilliant, all in the same match. I remember an experienced French rugby guy told me: 'If the French had the Anglo-Saxon mentality, they would be the best rugby players in the world.'

Derek: Do you speak any French? Or, come to that, any Spanish or Italian?

Ed: Very little. The first French team I refereed was Bordeaux University at Bristol University. I was very naive. Before the match, I asked them if anyone spoke English. '*Non, non,*' they said, and my refereeing wasn't good that day. Afterwards there were speeches and presentations, and the Bordeaux captain stood up and spoke fluent English. So that was a lesson learnt! Next time I did my preparation in advance. Found out, discreetly, who spoke English. Had a quiet word, and asked him to interpret on the field if we had a problem. In international matches, Frank Mesnel was a great help like that. So was Jean-Baptist Lafond.

Derek: It's the confidence factor again.

Ed: Exactly. If you trust each other, nothing's impossible. And I try to master a few brief phrases, because players respect the fact that you actually try to speak their language, even if you do it badly.

Derek: And I'm told that 'offside' means offside anywhere in the world.

Ed: Good!

A WHOLE NEW BALLGAME

Derek: There's an interesting cultural difference between British and American rugby. We use the tackle to defend. They use it to attack.

Ed: Yes, and to gain ground. Americans are fantastic tacklers. It's one of the disciplines they bring from American football. They'll drive the ball-carrier back and back. They use the tackle as a positive means of playing the game.

Derek: You may also have seen them using players to do what they call 'cleaning out the fringes' at rucks or mauls. If a guy's hanging around a ruck or maul he's liable to be bulldozed into the background by an opponent.

Ed: Called 'scatter-rucking', and it worries me. In American football it's legal to clear a patch for the ball-carrier, so scatter-rucking almost comes naturally to them. But it's the opposite of rugby, it's illegal, because cleaning the fringes is taking out a man without the ball.

Derek: And the guy doing the cleaning must be offside too.

Ed: Exactly. It's potentially dangerous – the player he takes out isn't expecting to be hit, and he could well get bashed in a vulnerable part, like the spleen or the kidneys. Immediately, that creates a flashpoint situation. Next thing you know, there's a fight.

Derek: All because that guy got into the act.

Ed: Cause and effect. Once the referee allows players to clean the fringes, he's handed over control of that part of the game, which is something he must never do. The referee must always control the players. I tell players, 'If anyone's fringing I'll penalise him. You don't take the law into your own hands.' That's absolutely essential to avoid flashpoints. And depending on the culture in different parts of the world, flashpoints can be more or less explosive.

Derek: Really? Where, for instance?

Ed: Well, the South Seas is not like Europe. In somewhere like Tonga or Fiji, or even Hawaii, it's part of their culture to look after the family. If they see one of the family being hard done by, their culture doesn't tell them to let the referee sort it out. Their culture says: *Get in there and start swinging!* Now, if you're going to referee those teams you need to have a little sympathy for their culture, or you'll never understand their game.

Derek: But you can't let their culture take over, surely.

Ed: No. Their way of solving problems leads to mayhem. What I'm saying is that rugby isn't just one game. It takes different forms in different countries. While we're locked in our cosy little environment, we don't realise that other people have totally different ideas about what's acceptable or unacceptable.

Derek: Did somebody mention replacement and substitution?

Ed: They've become an integral part of the game, haven't they? And their impact on how it's played is far greater than anyone anticipated. The lawmakers have done their best to keep control of the number of players leaving and entering the field of play, but . . . The hard fact is that up to seven players may be replaced/substituted, not counting the Blood Replacement/

Reversals coming and going; and many people believe that this isn't necessarily improving rugby as a game or a spectacle.

Derek: It's a far cry from the days when everyone knew that the result depended on 15 men and no more.

Ed: Replacement for injury – I can see that. But changing half your playing strength? That's excessive.

Derek: Rugby's problem is it's trying to satisfy a bunch of different cultures.

Ed: I'm always amazed at the silence at Twickenham when the visiting team kicks at goal. In other countries the spectators think they have a duty to shout and whistle and blow bugles to put off the kicker. And why not? That's their culture.

Derek: And then there's Japan.

Ed: Oh! Marvellous. I refereed Japan against Scotland, in the '91 World Cup. A fantastic occasion. They're tremendously inventive. They have great handling skills – speed at getting the ball back into play, and speed at moving it around the field, so they score some terrific tries.

Derek: But they always suffer at the line-out.

Ed: Not always. They've worked out some smart techniques for winning the ball, often by throwing it in as soon as they can. The Japanese never relax for a second. A lot of opponents are worried by the Japanese line-out because it happens so fast. The instant the guys line up, the ball's in, the line-out's over! No rest. But they'll avoid line-outs if they can. They don't want to kick their penalties to touch. They'd sooner tap and run! With their incredible hands, and their discipline, they're a sheer pleasure to referee.

Derek: When you say 'discipline', do you mean respect for the laws, or for you?

Ed: Both, really. Japanese culture is such that their respect for authority is greater than ours, and they see the referee as the man in authority. So there's never a problem.

Derek: Pure rugby.

Ed: Exactly. The nice thing is knowing that when they go out, they're going to do nothing else but play pure rugby. And that's a thing I enjoy.

Tailpiece

Derek: We're nearly at the end. Any last words of wisdom for the new referee?

Ed: Well . . . this might not be what the Powers That Be want to hear.

Derek: Good. Fire ahead.

Ed: I've never made any bones about the fact that I only referee because I can't play. Not strictly true, because even after I took up the whistle, I managed to fit in the odd game. I'd been playing rugby since I was ten. Hard to accept the end was in sight. Very hard.

Derek: Let's be clear here. You've played while you were a referee?

Ed: Many times. If the match I'd been appointed to referee was cancelled, I went along to my club and played in the 4th XV or whatever. Thoroughly enjoyed it. In the early days, some of the lords and masters of the refereeing world were saying to me, 'You'd better make your mind up! Because this is going to affect your career opportunities . . .'

Derek: It's certainly unusual for a referee to go on playing.

Ed: I believed that playing the game was actually helping my refereeing. It was keeping me in contact with the playing side. And I believe that referees need to understand as much as possible about play and players.

Derek: No substitute for experience, and so on.

Ed: It's a cliché, but that doesn't stop it being true. The more you've played, the better you understand the players. If someone's tugged your shirt, you know what it does to your mind. You have a feel for the action, and the reaction. What worries me is that we're now getting people who decide they're not going to make a very good rugby player, so they quit playing and see if they can make a very good referee instead.

Derek: It's true. Referees and policemen get younger every year.

Ed: Well, I'm old-fashioned enough to think that you play for as long as you can play, and then you referee. I look at these very young referees, and I wonder. We can give them books and videos, we can coach them and send them to conferences – but is that an adequate substitute for the natural understanding you get from playing a lot of rugby?

Derek: These young referees are very keen, very hard-working. They're very good technically.

Ed: The more you've played, the better you'll referee, because you'll have a wider understanding of the players – how they act and react. If someone's tugged your shirt, you'll know what it does to your mind.

Ed: I don't doubt it. What I'm not so sure is whether they'll have the depth of understanding to deal with the real pressure situations.

Derek: So your advice to a young referee is . . . ?

Ed: Go back and play. As I said, I only referee because I can't play. Playing comes first, and second, and third. If you can't play, then by all means referee. But the more you've played, the better you'll referee. We exist to help the players play. It's not easy. I certainly don't find refereeing easy. I have to work at it for eighty minutes.

Derek: Somebody said that being a rugby referee is the most demanding job in sport.

Ed: That's what makes it so satisfying.

Index